Bridge to IELTS

Pre-intermediate–Intermediate Band 3.5 to 4.5

Student's Book

Louis Harrison
Susan Hutchison

Australia • Brazil • Japan • Korea • Mexico • Singapore • Spain • United Kingdom • United States

Bridge to IELTS Student's Book

Louis Harrison and Susan Hutchison

Publisher: Jason Mann

Senior Commissioning Editor: John Waterman

Editorial Project Manager: Karen White

Development Editor: Carole Hughes

Head of Marketing and Communications:
  Michelle Cresswell

Project Editor: Denise Power

Production Controller: Elaine Willis

Art Director: Natasa Arsenidou

Cover design: Natasa Arsenidou

Text design: Andrew Oliver

Compositor: Maria Papageorgiou

Audio: Soundhouse studios, London

ISBN: 978-1-133-31894-1

National Geographic Learning
Cheriton House, North Way, Andover, Hampshire, SP10 5BE
United Kingdom

Cengage Learning is a leading provider of customised learning solutions with office locations around the globe, including Singapore, the United Kingdom, Australia, Mexico, Brazil and Japan. Locate our local office at **international.cengage.com/region**

Cengage Learning products are represented in Canada by Nelson Education Ltd.

Visit National Geographic Learning online at **ngl.cengage.com**
Visit our corporate website at **www.cengage.com**

CREDITS

Although every effort has been made to contact copyright holders before publication, this has not always been possible. If contacted, the publisher will undertake to rectify and errors or omissions at the earliest opportunity.

Photos

The publisher would like to thank the following sources for permission to reproduce their copyright protected photographs:

Alamy pp6 t (Tetra Images), 9 tl (Enigma), 10 b (Louise Heusinkveld), 10 c (Elizabeth Whiting & Associates), 14 br (Rubens Abboud), 14 cl (Hemis), 14 cr (Hemis), 14 tl (Peter Adams Photography Ltd), 14 tr (Hemis), 15 (STOCK4B GmbH), 16 A (Travelscape Images), 19 (Philip Scalia), 20 A (Simon Reddy), 20 B (Thomas Cockrem), 20 D (Chad Ehlers), 24 t (Stockbroker), 25 r (Ian Shaw), 26 b (Ellis Nature), 26 c (Martin Harvey), 27 (Marvin Dembinsky Photo Associates), 30 C (Robert Harding Picture Library Ltd), 36 (WoodyStock), 40 (Image Source), 42 t (Arcaid Images), 43 B, 47 b (Iain Masterton), 47 t (Mihail Chekalov), 48 A (Bill Bachmann), 48 B (Ilya Genkin), 48 C (Lebrecht Music and Arts Photo Library), 49 r (Gianni Muratore), 51 b (Ian Canham), 51 t (David L. Moore - CA10), 53 cr (Peter Titmuss), 55 b (Barry Mason), 55 t (Gianni Muratore), 56 A (Jeff Greenberg), 56 B (Stockfolio), 56 C (Hemis), 56 D (Danita Delimont), 57 l (Ros Drinkwater), 58 b (Tibor Bognar), 59 br (Y H Lim), 60 t (Christophe Diesel Michot), 61 bl (ZUMA Press, Inc.), 64 t (Sergey Goruppa), 66 cr (Tony Rolls), 69 t (Action Plus Sports Images), 73 r (WILDLIFE GmbH), 74 cl (amana images inc.), 76 cr (Bon Appetit), 78 l (Pin Xiao), 78 r (Joan Pollock), 79 (Robert Harding Picture Library Ltd), 80 (DWC), 81 (Chris Willson), 82 bl (Cops), 82 br (Marjorie Kamys Cotera/Bob Daemmrich Photography), 82 tr (amana images inc.), 83 c (BlueMoon Stock), 83 r (TongRo Image Stock), 85 (Tetra Images), 86 br (Jim West), 86 t (Juniors Bildarchiv), 89 (Tim Gainey), 90 E (Kenneth Edward Lewis), 93 t (Photoshot Holdings Ltd), 95 b (Jim West), 96 3 (Simon Hadley), 96 4 (China Images), 96 bl (Jim West), 99 b (Avesun), 100 tl (Jan Kozelnicky), 102 bl (Leila Cutler), 105 (Photofusion Picture Library), 106 l (Michael Schmeling), 106 r (Roger Bamber), 109 (67photo), 110 b (Andalucia Plus Image bank), 112 tl (itanistock), 113 (Rolf Richardson), 114 r (amana images inc.), 122 r (Greg Bajor | Images), 125 (Rupert Sagar-Musgrave), 126 l (Simon Kolton) **Corbis UK Ltd.** pp9 b (Owen Franken), 52 (Richard Ransier), 66 cl (Ocean) **Fotoe** pp76 t (Chen Yong), 127 **Fotolia** p117 cr (Enigmatico) **Getty Images** pp16 C (Ryan McVay), 16 D (Steve Allen), 24 bl (Steve Prezant), 26 t (Konrad Wothe), 30 A (Clive Brunskill), 30 B (Sean Gallup), 30 D (Munawar Hosain/Fotos International), 32 12 (Elie Bernager), 32 t (Assembly), 33 cr (Celia Peterson), 33 tr (Image Source), 50 (PhotoAlto/James Hardy), 53 bl (David Leahy), 63 b (Cameron Spencer), 66 br (Imagemore Co. Ltd.), 68 b (Rodney Hyett), 69 b (Jochen Schlenker), 74 bl (Dreaming life), 74 cr (Buyenlarge), 76 cl (Will Heap), 87 (Stephen Simpson), 94 t (Kevork Djansezian), 99 c (Justin Sullivan), 102 b (Design Pics/Ron Nickel), 110 t (Ian Walton), 115 r (Daly and Newton), 116 r (Richard Ross), 117 tl; **Linn Lönroth** p42 B, 42 C **Maria Papageorgiou** pp27, 69 **Martin Banfield** p84 **Mary Evans Picture Library** p45 b (Alinari Archives) **Muji** p99 t **Press Association Images** pp72 b (AP Photo/Olivier Asselin), 98 c (PA WIRE) **Reality Rush**, LLC p61 t **Rex Features** pp43 A (Hufton + Crow / View Pictures), 43 C; 61 br (Paul Brown), 96 br (KPA/Zuma), 98 t (Jonathan Hordle), 100 tcr (Glenn Copus / Evening Standard) **Shutterstock** pp6 b (Andresr), 6 bl (Mr. Lightman), 6 cr (Graphic design), 7 cr (Nataliia Natykach), 10 t (gh19), 13 (LeniKovaleva), 14 c (glyph), 16 b (Aleksandr Bryliaev), 16 tc (Oleksii Sagitov), 16 tl (Subbotina Anna), 18 t (maximma), 20 C (Jordan Tan), 21 (timothy passmore), 24 b (Adam Wasilewski), 24 br (Piotr Marcinski), 24 cr (Maksym Bondarchuk), 28 (Anton Gvozdikov), 29 (Goodluz), 32 1 (gualtiero boffi), 32 10 (nmedia), 32 6 (ronstik), 32 9 (vladek), 33 bl (wavebreakmedia ltd),33 c (Nicemonkey), 33 cl (shock), 33 tl (Jaimie Duplass), 33 tl (hxdbzxy), 35 (Andresr), 41 (jayfish), 45 t (Alice), 49 l (kenny1), 54 t (Dmitry Kalinovsky), 57 r (Monkey Business Images), 58 t (Aleksandr Bryliaev), 60 b (Mona Redshinestudio), 60 c (humpkin), 63 t (Loskutnikov), 71 cl (Brux), 71 cr (Ermek), 72 t (One And Only), 74 tr (Hiroshi Ichikawa), 76 b (Discpicture), 76 c (Mushakesa), 86 bl (vlavetal), 90 A (Jason Prince), 92 br (prism68), 92 cr (Armin Rose), 92 tl (Dragana Gerasimoski), 94 b (Umberto Shtanzman), 95 t (David M. Schrader), 96 1 (yykkaa), 96 5 (jiawangkun), 97 b (Triff), 97 t (caesart), 100 b (franco's photos), 100 bc (REDAV), 100 bl (iStockphoto), 103 b (Sean Reilly), 103 c (Nataly-Nete), 103 l (Timea), 103 t (pakowacz), 106 b (Excellent backgrounds), 106 t (Nicemonkey), 112 c (Nicemonkey), 112 tr (Palmer Kane LLC), 114 l (Warren Goldswain), 114 t (magnola), 116 b (Nicemonkey), 116 l (1000 Words), 116 t (ruslanchik), 117 bl (sniegirova mariia), 117 c (Nicemonkey), 119 l (Timothy Epp), 119 r (Lasse Kristensen), 126 r (Dreamie) **Thinkstock** pp8 (Ryan McVay), 9 tr (BananaStock), 11 (iStockphoto), 16 B (Jupiterimages), 24 cl (iStockphoto), 25 l (Hemera), 31 (Jupiterimages), 32 11 (iStockphoto), 32 2 (Hemera), 32 3 (iStockphoto), 32 4 (Hemera), 32 5 (iStockphoto), 32 7 (iStockphoto), 32 8 (TongRo Image Stock), 37 (Medioimages/Photodisc), 42 A (iStockphoto), 53 tr (Jochen Sand), 54 b (Jupiterimages), 59 bl (Hemera), 59 tl (Hemera Technologies), 59 tr (iStockphoto), 64 b (Photodisc), 65 b (iStockphoto), 65 t (Comstock), 66 tl (iStockphoto), 66 tr (Goodshoot), 68 t (Digital Vision), 75 (Medioimages/Photodisc), 82 tl (iStockphoto), 90 B (Jupiterimages), 90 C (iStockphoto), 90 D (Anup Shah), 92 cl (iStockphoto), 93 bl (Ingram Publishing), 93 br (iStockphoto), 96 2 (Hemera), 98 b (Hemera Technologies), 102 bc (Jack Hollingsworth), 102 t (Jupiterimages), 108 (iStockphoto), 112 br (Hemera), 115 l (Jack Hollingsworth), 122 l (iStockphoto) **Zooid Pictures** p100 tr

Text

The publisher would like to thank the following sources for permission to reproduce their copyright protected texts:

Reality Rush LLC for details on page 60 about Urban Hunt, http://www.realityrush.com. Reproduced with permission; Weddingsday.co.uk for statistics on page 83 from 'Average UK Wedding day costs' http://www.weddingsday.co.uk/average-wedding-cost/. Reproduced with permission; and Wikipedia for chart on page 125 "Annual Greenhouse Gas Emissions by Sector" by Robert A. Rohde, http://en.wikipedia.org/wiki/File:Greenhouse_Gas_by_Sector.png. Granted under the Creative Commons Attribution-Share Alike 3.00 Unported License.

Illustrations by: Kees pp12, 18, 22, 26, 38, 39, 58, 62, 64, 65, 67, 71, 88, 101, 103, 104, 110, 113, 118, 119, 120, 121, 123, 125, 126, 127

Printed in China by RR Donnelley
1 2 3 4 5 6 7 8 9 10 – 16 15 14 13 12

Welcome to the *Bridge to IELTS* Student's Book!

Bridge to IELTS is the first stage in helping you prepare for taking the IELTS test. We want to help you improve your English language and test skills and also develop your study skills. We have carefully selected interesting topics and developed the language study step by step. We have also included revision sections to help you remember grammar and vocabulary you learned earlier.

At the same time as you improve your English language and study skills you'll get lots of test practice. Most of the activities in the units are based on real IELTS test question types so when you're improving your English skills, you're preparing for the test at the same time.

To make sure you're really ready to study for the test, in *Bridge to IELTS* boxes we've included information on how the test works as well as tips on how to do your best in the test.

And there's more! In *Bridge to IELTS* we help you understand the situations which feature in the test – student life and academic traditions that you will listen to and speak about in the test. Look out for the *Living IELTS* boxes which contain words and phrases to help you sound natural and confident.

Most of all, we hope that you enjoy the course and find it interesting, fun and motivating because we learn best when we enjoy what we're learning!

All good wishes

Louis Harrison and Susan Hutchison

Bridge to IELTS Course map

Key: Reading (R); Speaking (S); Listening (L); Writing (W)

READING

1 Complete the dialogue. Use the words below.

> fine Hello How meet new
> Nice student this well from

Ana: ¹ _____, Sergei!

Sergei: Hi, Ana! ² _____ are you?

Ana: I'm ³ _____, thanks. And you?

Sergei: I'm very ⁴ _____, thanks.

Ana: Sergei ⁵ _____ is Eva. She's from Argentina.

Eva: Hello, Sergei. ⁶ _____ to meet you.

Sergei: Nice to ⁷ _____ you too! I'm ⁸ _____ Russia.

Eva: Are you a ⁹ _____ student?

Sergei: Yes, I am.

Eva: I'm a new ¹⁰ _____ too!

2 🔊 1.1 **Listen and check your answers. Then work in groups of three and practise the dialogue.**

3 Read the text and answer the questions.

1 How many universities are there in Australia?
2 Who is O-week for?

4 Read the text again and choose Y (yes) or N (no).

1 Is Australia a young country? Y / N
2 Is O-week in the second week of
  the academic year? Y / N
3 Are some students from other countries? Y / N
4 Are the host students new students? Y / N

| Home | Faculties | A-Z Directory | Links |

STUDY IN AUSTRALIA

There are many reasons to study here! Australia is a very young and exciting country. There are 41 universities here and so there are many different courses to choose from! The teachers and the students are very friendly. Are you from another country? Don't worry! Many students here aren't from Australia either. They're from many different countries too.

The first week of the academic year at our universities is O-week. It's a time to meet people, make friends and have fun! O-week isn't a time to study! Student hosts are here to help you. They are students who know the university well. So ... Australia is a great place for you to live and learn! Australia is THE place to be!

LISTENING

1 🔘 1.2 **Listen to two students, Fouad and Agnes, talking at the O-Week meeting. Tick the things they talk about.**

A weather ☐   **D** family ☐
B food ☐   **E** friends ☐
C clothes ☐

2 🔘 1.2 **Listen again and choose the correct answers.**

1 Fouad is in the ... department.
  a science   **b** business   **c** art

2 Fouad and Agnes are in ...
  a Australia.   **b** Canada.   **c** Germany.

3 Yibo is from ...
  a China.   **b** Japan.   **c** Saudi Arabia.

4 The barbeque is on ...
  a Thursday.   **b** Friday.   **c** Saturday.

Living IELTS

INTRODUCING PEOPLE

🔘 1.3 **Listen and put the sentences in order.**

☐   Hello, Fouad. Nice to meet you too.
☐   Hi, Yibo. Nice to meet you.
☐   Fouad, this is Yibo. Yibo, this is Fouad. Yibo's a science student too.

Work in groups of three. Introduce each other.

GRAMMAR

PRESENT SIMPLE OF BE

You use the verb _be_ to give information about yourself, other people, things and places.

Australia **is** a very young and exciting country.
O-week **isn't** a time to study.
The teachers and the students **are** friendly.
Many students **aren't** from Australia.
**Are you** from another country?

The form of _be_ is different for different personal pronouns.

_**I am**_
You / we / they **are**
He / she / it **is**

📖 **GRAMMAR REFERENCE PAGE 138**

1 **Complete with the correct form of _be_.**

1 Berlin _____ in Germany. It's the capital city.
2 Fouad and Yibo _____ in Melbourne.
3 They _____ (not) in the art department.
4 I _____ (not) from Australia.
5 Agnes _____ (not) from Australia.
6 She _____ from Germany.

2 **Put the words in order to make questions.**

1 German / he / Is ?
2 Are / a / student / new / you ?
3 she / from / China / Is ?
4 they / Are / the / tour / on ?
5 Yibo / Is / your / name ?

3 **Complete the answers using the words below. Then match the answers with the questions in activity 2.**

are   aren't   isn't   It's   She's

a Yes, I _____. My name's Fouad.
b Yes, she is. _____ from Beijing.
c No, it isn't. _____ Agnes.
d No, he _____. He's Saudi.
e Yes, they _____. It's their first day at university!

PRONUNCIATION

VOWEL SOUNDS - /ɒ/ /eɪ/ /aɪ/

1 🔘 1.4 **Listen and match the words with the sounds.**

1	what	**a**	/aɪ/
2	name	**b**	/ɒ/
3	I	**c**	/eɪ/

2 🔘 1.5 **Listen and put the words in the table.**

/ɒ/	/eɪ/	/aɪ/

3 **Practise saying the words.**

VOCABULARY

MAKING FRIENDS

1 **Match the words to make phrases.**

1	chat	**a**	yourself to someone
2	meet	**b**	hello
3	say	**c**	a conversation
4	start	**d**	people
5	go out	**e**	to someone
6	introduce	**f**	with friends

2 **Complete the sentences using phrases from activity 1.**

1 It's easy to _____ when you meet someone for the first time. You say your name!

2 I _____ or Hi when I meet friends in the street.

3 You can _____ with someone by smiling, saying hello and making eye contact.

4 I _____ at the weekends – we go to the cinema or go shopping.

5 If you _____ you talk in a friendly, informal way with them.

6 Clubs are good places to _____ and have fun.

READING

1 **Match the pictures with the words below.**

sports club   Internet   band   choir

2 **Read the text and number the pictures in activity 1 in the order they are mentioned.**

Making friends

Are you someone who wants to make friends? Yes? Well ... read on!

A There are new people to meet everywhere – the person who is next to you in a class or someone who is in front of you in the lunch line. There are many different ways to start a conversation
5 with someone new, but it is always a good idea to smile and make eye contact before you begin. Just say 'hello' and ask questions like, 'Where are you from?'. The weather is always a good topic for conversation. You can say, 'It's a nice day, isn't
10 it?'. It's important to keep the conversation light and it's also a good idea to follow a 30/70 pattern during small talk when possible. This is 30% talking and 70% listening.

B The Internet is a great way to get to know
15 people and make friends. It isn't always
necessary for friends to have common
interests. Some good friends are people who
are very different from each other! However,
it's easy to spend a lot of time online with
20 someone who you think is a friend and then
find there's no chance to meet them because
of time and distance.

C Sports clubs are great places to keep healthy
and make friends at the same time. They are
25 not just for people who are good at playing a
sport – they are for everyone. The important
thing is to enjoy what you do and have fun.
A sports team isn't the only way to a good
social life. If you play a musical instrument or
30 sing, there are bands or choirs you can join too.

3 Choose T (true) or F (false).

1 There are two ways to start a conversation. T / F
2 It is a good idea to talk about serious topics
when you meet someone new. T / F
3 It is more important to listen than to talk. T / F
4 Most good friends are very different from
each other. T / F
5 The Internet is not always a good way to
make friends. T / F
6 A sports team is the best way to meet new
friends. T / F

4 Read the text again and circle TWO answers.

1 When you meet someone new it is important to …
a smile.
b laugh.
c make eye contact.

2 Good places to get to know new people are …
a not easy to find.
b online.
c clubs.

3 Sports clubs are …
a fun.
b for everyone.
c for people who like team sports only.

**5 Find the words in the text and choose the correct
meaning.**

1 *Small talk* (line 12) is …
a polite conversation about everyday things like
the weather.
b conversation about serious topics.

2 A *common interest* (line 16) is …
a an activity which you share with another
person.
b an activity you like to do by yourself.

3 If you live at a *distance* (line 22) from something,
you live …
a far.
b near.

4 If you have *a good social life* (line 28) you are …
a usually at home by yourself.
b often out with people and having fun.

Discussion

Work in pairs. Ask and answer the questions.

1 Which is the best way to make friends? Why?
2 What do you talk about when you meet new people?

VOCABULARY

ADJECTIVES TO DESCRIBE ROOMS

1 **Match the pictures with the words below.**

> flat   house   student hall   bedsit

2 **Look at the words below. Which can you use to describe the following things?**

> big   bright   cold   uncomfortable
> comfortable   noisy   small   tidy
> warm   quiet   dark

- a chair
- a bed
- a room
- a house or flat

3 **Put the words in activity 2 in pairs of opposites. Which word has no opposite?**

4 **Choose the correct answers.**

1 It's a very hard chair – it's very *comfortable /
uncomfortable*.
2 There's a lot of light in this room – it's very *dark /
bright*.
3 It's very *quiet / noisy* near her flat. It's next to a
busy road.
4 It's a very *small / large* flat so there isn't much
space.
5 Her flat isn't very *tidy / cold*. Her books are
everywhere!
6 It's very *cold / warm* in here. Can I open the
window?

Discussion

**Work in pairs. Which place in the photos would
you most like to live in? Why?**

LISTENING

1 🔘 1.6 **Listen to Hassan and Etsuko talking about where they live. Choose the correct answers.**

1 Hassan is talking to a student from …
  a Egypt.
  b Japan.
  c Australia.

2 His home is …
  a near the university.
  b far from the university.
  c at the university.

3 Etsuko is in a …
  a student hall.
  b house.
  c flat.

4 There is a … near her home.
  a park
  b shopping centre
  c station

2 🔘 1.6 **Listen again and tick the things they mention.**

bed	☐	bookshelves	☐	desk	☐
lamp	☐	sofa	☐	table	☐
window	☐	laptop	☐		

④

GRAMMAR

THERE IS / THERE ARE

You use *there is* with singular nouns and *there are* with plural nouns.

There is *a sofa.* **There *isn't*** *a desk.*
There are *three rooms.* **There *aren't*** *bookshelves.*
Is there *a desk? Yes,* ***there is****. / No,* ***there isn't****.*
Are there *bookshelves? Yes,* ***there are****. / No,* ***there aren't****.*

📖 **GRAMMAR REFERENCE PAGE 138**

1 **Choose the correct words.**

1 *There is / There are* a table in Hassan's room.
2 *There is / There are* a sofa in Hassan's room.
3 *There is / There are* a park near Etsuko's home.
4 *There is / There are* three rooms in Hassan's flat.

2 **Complete the questions with *Is there / Are there*.**

1 _____ three people in Hassan's room?
2 _____ a lot of noise in Etsuko's room?
3 _____ a laptop in Hassan's room?
4 _____ bookshelves in Etsuko's room?

3 **Put the words in order to make questions.**

1 big / window / there / Is / your / room / in / a ?
2 there / Are / shops / home / near / your ?
3 your / home / Is / quiet / very ?
4 it / to / place / live / Is / a / good ?

4 **Complete the answers with the words below. Then match the answers with the questions in activity 3.**

is   There's   isn't   there

a Yes, there are. _____ a big shopping centre.
b Yes, it _____. It's right in the centre of the city.
c Yes, _____ is. There's a lovely view.
d No, it _____. It's very noisy.

5 **Work in pairs. Ask and answer the questions in activity 3.**

SPEAKING

DESCRIBING A ROOM

1 **Work in pairs. Ask and answer the questions.**

1 Where do you like to study?
- at home
- in a library
- somewhere else

2 When do you like to study?
- in the morning
- in the afternoon
- in the evening

3 How do you like to study?
- on your own
- with other people

2 🔊 **1.7 Listen to Marisa talking about where she likes to study. Which picture is Marisa's room?**

3 🔊 **1.7 Listen again and choose the correct answers.**

1 Marisa's room is …
   a small.   **b** big.   **c** quiet.

2 She thinks the colour blue is …
   a calm.   **b** warm.   **c** cold.

3 There … in the room.
   a are three bookshelves **b** are two bookshelves
   c is a red chair

4 The room is a good place to study in because …
   a it's noisy.   **b** it's quiet.   **c** it's bright.

4 **Think about your ideal room to study in. Make notes about it. Think about …**
- where it is.
- what colour the room is.
- what there is in the room.
- why it is a good room to study in.

Bridge to IELTS

STARTING YOUR TALK

A good way to start your talk is to repeat the words on the card. *My ideal room to study in? My ideal room to study in is …* Say these words slowly and clearly. This gives you time to think about what you can say next.

5 **Work in pairs. Take turns to talk about the topic card. Use the notes you made in activity 4 to help you.**

Describe your ideal room to study in.

You should say:
- where the room is
- what colour the room is
- what there is in the room
  and say why it is a good place to study in.

Writing

A personal description

1 **Look at the picture. Guess which of these sentences describe the city.**

1 It's a big city.
2 There are shops.
3 There isn't a cinema.
4 There are restaurants.
5 It's in the centre of the city.
6 It's a good place to live.

2 **Read the text and check your answers.**

My name's Natalia. I'm from Novgorod. It's a small city in the west of Russia. My flat is in the centre of the city. There are lots of shops, restaurants and cinemas near it. My flat is not very big but it's very comfortable, warm and bright. It's a great place to live!

Writing skills

Word order

3 **Put the words in order to make questions.**

1 name / your / What's ?
2 from / Where / you / are ?
3 your / Where / is / city ?
4 home / is / Where / your ?
5 is / home / near / your / What ?
6 is / like / What / home / your ?

4 **Write the answers to the questions for Natalia.**

5 **Answer the questions in activity 3 for you.**

6 **Complete the text for you. Use the notes you made in activity 5.**

My name's ^{1} _____ . I'm from
^{2} _____ . It's a ^{3} _____ .
My home is in ^{4} _____ . There are
^{5} _____ near it. My home is
^{6} _____ . It's a great place to live!

Unit 2
Festivals

HOME | HISTORY | PHOTO | VIDEOS | ABOUT US | CONTACT

Quebec Winter Carnival

Chantal lives in Quebec in Canada. She speaks English and French. Every year she goes to the Quebec Winter Carnival. It's one of the largest festivals in the world and many people visit the city for two weeks in January or February to enjoy it. They come to celebrate winter and go to fun attractions, including colourful street parades. Chantal loves the carnival! She likes looking at the snow sculptures but she doesn't want to touch them – they are too cold! There is also a canoe race across the icy St Lawrence River but don't come to watch it if you don't like cold weather! The carnival mascot is *Bonhomme*, a snowman in a red hat.

READING

1 **Work in pairs. Describe what you can see in the pictures. Use the words below.**

> canoe river snow sculpture snowman parade

2 **Read the webpage and answer the questions.**

1 When does the festival take place?
2 How long does it last?
3 What are the sculptures made of?
4 What is the name of the snowman?

3 **Choose the correct meaning for the words in the text.**

1 A *carnival* is …
  a a big party that takes place on the streets.
  b a dance show.

2 If you *enjoy* something you …
  a don't like it. **b** have a good time.

3 *Attractions* are …
  a things you buy. **b** things you look at.

4 An *icy* river is …
  a very cold. **b** very warm.

5 A *mascot* …
  a brings good luck. **b** brings bad luck.

GRAMMAR

PRESENT SIMPLE

You use the present simple to talk about things which are always or generally true.

It's one of the largest festivals in the world.

You also use the present simple to talk about habits or things you do regularly.

Every year she goes to the Quebec Winter Carnival.

The form of the present simple is the same for all personal pronouns, except the third person *he / she / it.*

I / You / We / They live in Quebec.
He / she / it lives in Quebec.

 GRAMMAR REFERENCE PAGE 138

1 Write the third-person form of the verbs below.

> come   enjoy   go   like   live
> say   speak   visit   want

2 Choose the correct answers.

1 I *like / don't like* winter! It's too cold!
2 She lives in Quebec and *doesn't go / goes* to the carnival every year.
3 'I *don't have / have* a hat to wear!' 'Don't worry! I can give you one!'
4 We *want / don't want* to watch the canoe race. It's fun and exciting!
5 They *speak / don't speak* two languages in Quebec – English and French.

3 Complete the text. Use the correct form of the words below.

> enjoy   come   last   look
> take place   want   watch

People from all over Canada ¹ _____ to the Quebec Winter Festival. It ² _____ every year in January and ³ _____ for two weeks. They ⁴ _____ to celebrate winter and ⁵ _____ many different attractions. They ⁶ _____ at beautiful snow sculptures and ⁷ _____ the famous canoe race.

Discussion

Complete the sentence for you. Then work in pairs and compare your sentences.

I *want / don't want* to go to the Quebec Winter Carnival because …

LISTENING

1 〔1.8〕 **Listen to two students, Etsuko and Ahmed, talking about the Quebec Winter Carnival. Circle the correct answers.**

1 The carnival starts on …
   a Saturday.   **b** Sunday.   **c** Thursday.

2 Etsuko really wants to see …
   a the canoe race.   **b** the ice palace.
   c the snow bath.

3 Ahmed likes …
   a watching sport.   **b** cold weather.
   c playing sport.

4 He doesn't have …
   a a hat.   **b** gloves.   **c** a scarf.

2 〔1.8〕 **Listen again and choose T (true) or F (false).**

1 Ahmed likes winter.   T / F
2 Etsuko doesn't like the weather in Canada.   T / F
3 Ahmed doesn't want to see the ice palace.   T / F
4 Ahmed doesn't want to watch the canoe race. T / F
5 Etsuko wants to have a bath in the snow.   T / F

Living IELTS

TALKING ABOUT LIKES AND DISLIKES

〔1.9〕 **Listen and mark the stress in the sentences.**

I really don't like winter.
I love it.
I like playing sport.
I hate watching sport in the cold!

〔1.9〕 **Listen again and practise.**

VOCABULARY

POSITIVE AND NEGATIVE ADJECTIVES

1 Look at the adjectives below. Which have a positive meaning and which have a negative meaning? Put + or – next to each adjective.

awful _____
interesting _____
exciting _____
beautiful _____
colourful _____
fantastic _____
amazing _____
boring _____
freezing _____
delicious _____

2 Work in pairs. Answer the questions.

1 Which adjective can you use to describe good food?

2 Which two adjectives mean 'very good'?

3 Which adjective can you use to describe something very bad?

4 Which adjective can you use to describe something very cold?

3 Choose the correct word.

1 Mmm! This cake is *delicious / awful*.

2 The weather is perfect today! It's *beautiful / colourful*.

3 You need to put a coat on before you go outside. It's *fantastic / freezing*.

4 The end of the race is always interesting to watch. It's very *exciting / awful*.

5 I think that's a *fantastic / awful* idea. Let's go to the carnival together!

6 These snow sculptures are *boring / amazing*! Each one is different.

4 Choose the odd one out.

1 awful	amazing	fantastic
2 interesting	awful	boring
3 fantastic	delicious	freezing
4 colourful	beautiful	awful

5 Complete the sentences for you.

1 I think _____ is delicious.

2 I think snow sculptures are _____.

3 I think winter is _____.

4 I think canoe races are _____.

5 I think the snowman is _____.

PRONUNCIATION

SYLLABLE STRESS

1 Match the words with the number of syllables.

1 festival	**a**	2
2 winter	**b**	3
3 attraction	**c**	3

2 🔊 1.10 Listen and put the words in the table.

Oo	Ooo	oOo
winter	festival	attraction

3 Practise saying the words.

READING

1 Work in pairs. Look at the photographs A-D. What can you see? Tick the phrases below.

barbeque on the beach ☐   masquerade party ☐
firework display ☐   picnic in the park ☐

2 ⏱(3min) Read the passage in three minutes. Number the pictures in the order they are mentioned in the passage.

3 Read the passage again and answer the questions.

1 When is New Year's Day?
2 How do Australians spend New Year's Eve?
3 In which two cities do the largest New Year celebrations take place?
4 How many people watch the firework display in Sydney?
5 Why are fireworks important in New Year celebrations?

4 Complete with words from the passage.

1 c_____: show that a day or event is important by doing something special (paragraph A)
2 e_____: something that is interesting and fun to watch (paragraph B)
3 m_____: very big (paragraph C)
4 i_____: very big or attractive (paragraph D)

Discussion

Work in pairs. Discuss the questions.

1 Are the New Year celebrations in Australia similar or different to the way people celebrate New Year in your country?
2 Would you like to celebrate New Year in Australia? Why / Why not?

New Year IN AUSTRALIA

A Many Australians celebrate New Year's Eve on 31 December each year. It is the day before New Year's Day, the 1 January. New Year's Eve is not a public holiday in Australia but schools and colleges are closed because it is a holiday period. Some offices may also be closed because a lot of people don't go to work during this time.

B Many Australian cities have special New Year's Eve events that include parades, music and entertainment. Some people go to masquerade parties. Other people have picnics in parks or have special parties and barbeques in their own homes or on boats and beaches.

C The largest New Year's Eve celebrations take place in Sydney and Melbourne. In Sydney over 1.5 million people go to a massive firework display with around 5 000 fireworks let off from the bridge and from boats in the harbour.

D Firework displays mark the end of the old year and the beginning of the New Year. The largest and most impressive firework displays are at midnight on New Year's Eve. It is a way of saying goodbye to the past and saying hello to the future.

Listening

1 Label the picture with the words in the box. Then group the words under two headings: people and things.

> clown float stall kite musician
> puppet dancer acrobat

2 Read the poster and answer the questions.

1 What is the name of the festival? ☐
2 When is it? ☐
3 Where does it happen? ☐
4 What time does it start? ☐
5 How much does it cost? ☐

3 🔊 1.11 Listen to two friends, Fouad and Jing, talking about the Festival of the Winds. Tick the questions in activity 2 that they answer.

4 🔊 1.11 Listen again and choose TWO answers.

1 How often does the festival take place?
  a every spring
  b once a year
  c every two years

2 Who takes part in the festival?
  a kite fliers
  b kite makers only
  c people from all over the world

3 Which activity does Fouad want to do?
  a make a kite
  b watch a dance show
  c visit the food stalls

4 How do Fouad and Jing decide to go to the festival?
  a by car
  b by train
  c by bus

FESTIVAL of the WINDS

Sydney's most colourful kite flying festival

Sunday 9ᵗʰ September

11am–4pm Bondi Beach **FREE!**

GRAMMAR

PRESENT SIMPLE QUESTIONS AND SHORT ANSWERS

You form present simple questions with the auxiliary *do* or *does* and the base form of the verb.

Do I / you / we / they **live** in Australia? Yes, I / you / we / they **do**. No, I / you / we / they **don't**.

Does he / she / it **live** in Australia? Yes, he / she / it **does**. No, he / she / it **doesn't**.

 GRAMMAR REFERENCE PAGE 138

1 Choose the correct answers.

1 When you form *questions / negative sentences* in the present simple, you use the auxiliary verb *do* or *does*.

2 The auxiliary comes *before / after* the subject and the verb.

2 Complete the questions with *Do* or *Does*.

1 _____ you want to go to the festival?
2 _____ your teacher wear a red hat?
3 _____ the parades start here?
4 _____ we have food for the picnic?
5 _____ the race take place on the river?

3 Put the words in order to make questions.

1 French / you / speak / Do ?
2 have / she / Does / car / a ?
3 to / take / bus / want / the / they / Do ?
4 Sunday / the / start / Does / on / carnival ?
5 need / gloves / Do / some / I ?

4 Match the questions in activity 3 with the short answers.

1 Yes, they do.
2 No, you don't.
3 Yes, it does.
4 Yes, I do.
5 No, she doesn't.

Question words

Question word	Auxiliary	Subject	Verb
What	do	you	do?
When / Where / What time / Why	does	the parade	take place?
How long	do	they	last?
How much	does	the festival	cost?

 GRAMMAR REFERENCE PAGE 138

5 Choose the correct words.

1 *What / How* kind of food do you like?
2 *When / Where* do you live?
3 *What time / How long* does your English class start?
4 *When / How long* does your English class last?
5 *How much / Why* does a newspaper cost in your country?

6 Answer the questions in activity 5 for you.

7 Complete the questions for these answers about a festival.

1 _____ is it called? Mardi Gras.
2 _____ is it? In New Orleans.
3 _____ is it? In February.
4 _____ is it? Four days.
5 _____ happens? There are street parades and bands.

8 Work in pairs. Student A, turn to page 124. Student B, turn to page 126. Read the information. Then ask and answer the questions in activity 3 about the festivals.

Speaking

A SPECIAL DAY OR EVENT

1 **Work in pairs. Ask and answer the questions.**

  1 Does your country celebrate a national day? If so, when and how?

  2 Do you think that national days are important? Why? / Why not?

2 🔊 1.12 **Listen to Leah talking about National Day in Singapore. Number the pictures in the order she talks about them.**

3 🔊 1.12 **Listen again and answer the questions.**

  1 When is Singapore National Day?
    a 9 August
    b 19 August
    c 29 August

  2 Who does Leah celebrate the day with?
    a Her family only.
    b Her friends only.
    c Her family and friends.

  3 What does she do to celebrate?
    a She cooks for her friends.
    b She dances in a show.
    c She watches a parade.

  4 Why is it an important day for her?
    a She spends time with her family.
    b She wears national costume.
    c She remembers her country.

4 **Think of special day or event. Make notes about it. Think about …**

  • what it is.
  • when it is.
  • what you do.
  • why it is special for you.

Bridge to IELTS

TASK CARDS

In task 2 (individual long turn), the examiner gives you a task card to talk about, a pencil and some paper. You have one minute to think about the topic and make notes to help you talk.

5 **Work in pairs. Take turns to talk about the topic card. Use the notes you made in activity 4 to help you.**

Describe a special day or event.

You should say:
- what it is
- when it is
- what you do
and explain why it is special for you.

WRITING

DESCRIBING A FESTIVAL

1 Work in pairs. Look at the picture and guess the answers to the questions.

   1 Where is the festival?
     a London
     b Beijing
     c Cairo

   2 When does it happen?
     a in January
     b in August
     c in November

2 Read the text and check your answers to the questions in activity 1.

> The Notting Hill Carnival is a special festival in London, in the UK. It takes place in August and lasts two days. There are floats and colourful street parades with music and dancing. There are food stalls and people eat delicious food from all over the world. It is a special event because people from many different cultures go to the festival and it is fun.

WRITING SKILLS

PUNCTUATION

3 Read the text in activity 2 again. Complete the sentences with these words.

> full stop   months   capital letter   places

   1 You use a _____ at the beginning of a sentence.
   2 You use a _____ at the end of a sentence.
   3 You use capital letters for the names of _____, people, _____ and countries.

4 Rewrite the sentences with capital letters and full stops.

   1 my favourite festival takes place in thailand in april
   2 leah comes from singapore
   3 the festival doesn't happen in australia
   4 he always spends time in quebec in january

5 Think of a festival. Make notes about it in the table.

1 What is it?	
2 Where is it?	
3 When is it?	
4 How long does it last?	
5 What happens?	
6 What do people do?	
7 Why is it special?	

6 Complete the text. Use the notes you made in activity 5.

The ¹ _____ is a special festival in ² _____ . It takes place in ³ _____ and lasts ⁴ _____ . There are ⁵ _____ and people ⁶ _____ . It is a special event because ⁷ _____ .

Review Units 1 and 2

GRAMMAR

1 Work in pairs. Student A, look at the picture and make questions using the words below. Student B, turn to page 126 and answer Student A's questions. Find the differences in the pictures.

1 a red sofa? *Is there a red sofa?*
2 two small windows?
3 blue walls?
4 a laptop on the desk?
5 yellow lamp?
6 four bookshelves?
7 two beds?

2 Choose the correct form to complete the sentences.

Many Canadians celebrate New Year's Eve on 31 December – the day before the New Year ¹ *begin / begins* on 1st January. It is a holiday period so a lot of people ² *don't go / doesn't go* to work. Special events ³ *take place / takes place* in many big cities. Jon ⁴ *live / lives* in Toronto and ⁵ *watch / watches* a big firework display. Some people ⁶ *do / does* winter sports such as skiing and snowboarding. Jacques ⁷ *come / comes* from Quebec in Northern Canada. He ⁸ *spend / spends* the night ice-fishing on a frozen lake with his friends. He ⁹ *love / loves* cold weather!

3 Complete the questions with *do* or *does*. Then read the table and complete the sentences.

1 _____ Jon speak French?
2 _____ they like hot weather?
3 _____ Csilla like dogs?
4 _____ he live in Canada?
5 _____ she drive a black car?
6 _____ they study at weekends?

	Jon	Csilla
speak French?	✓	✗
enjoy sport?	✗	✓
come from a big city?	✓	✓
live in a flat?	✗	✓
like cold weather?	✓	✗
drive a black car?	✗	✓
study at weekends?	✗	✗

1 Jon ____ *speaks* ____ French.
2 He _____ sport.
3 Csilla _____ a black car.
4 She _____ cold weather.
5 They _____ at weekends.
6 He _____ in a flat.
7 They _____ from a big city.

4 Work in pairs. Ask and answer the same questions.

5 Read the table and complete the text with the correct form of the verbs in brackets.

Name	Ana
Nationality/city	Spanish, Madrid
Age	20
Home	flat
Occupation	student
Interests	sport (tennis and basketball), going out with friends
Languages	English and Spanish

Her name ¹ _____ (be) Ana and she is Spanish. She ² _____ (come) from Madrid, the capital of Spain. She ³ _____ (be) twenty years old and she ⁴ _____ (live) in a big flat near the city centre. She ⁵ _____ (study) engineering at university. She ⁶ _____ (like) sport; especially tennis and basketball. She also ⁷ _____ (enjoy) reading and going out with friends. Ana ⁸ _____ (speak) two languages – English and Spanish of course!

6 Now write about you!

Vocabulary

1 Match the adjectives with their opposites.

1 comfortable	a quiet
2 big	b dark
3 bright	c small
4 noisy	d warm
5 cold	e uncomfortable

2 Complete the sentences with the verbs below.

> chat   go out   introduce   meet   say   start

1 Sergei is a new student too. Why don't you _____ yourself to him?
2 How do you _____ a conversation with someone new? Do you talk about the weather?
3 I usually _____ with my friends at the weekends. We go to a club or watch a film.
4 Ana's over there. Let's go and _____ to her.
5 It's a really friendly sports club. It's a great place to _____ new people.
6 Do you _____ hello or hi when you meet friends in the street?

3 Complete the sentences with the words below.

> awful   boring   colourful   delicious
> fantastic   freezing

1 This chocolate tastes really good. It's _____.
2 What _____ weather! Let's stay here and watch a movie on TV!
3 Look at the ice on the lake! It's _____.
4 What a _____ idea! Let's go to the film together.
5 He's really dull and _____. He talks about the same things again and again.
6 Look at those fireworks! The sky is really _____!

4 Choose TWO adjectives.

1 It's a really *exciting / boring / interesting* book. I want to find out what happens at the end!
2 What a lovely dress! You look really *beautiful / awful / amazing* in it!
3 I love Japanese food. It's *fantastic / delicious / boring*.
4 Let's go to the parade. It's really *colourful / boring / beautiful* to watch.
5 This party is really *boring / interesting / awful*. I want to go home now.

Bridge to IELTS

TEST PREPARATION

1 **Work in pairs. Write three things you know about IELTS.**

2 **Read the passage and underline any new information.**

3 **Discuss your answers with the class.**

> **An international test**
> The International English Language Testing System is a test of English language skills in an academic situation. It takes two hours and fifty four minutes to complete. It does not directly test your grammar and vocabulary, but you need good grammar and vocabulary to get a good score. There are four parts to the test. The first part is listening, then reading followed by writing and finally speaking. Scores are from 0 (no English) to 9 (native-speaker English). *Bridge to IELTS* helps you prepare for all parts of the test.

4 **Work in pairs and answer the questions.**

1 What part of the test do you think you are good at?
2 Why would you like to take the test?

Study Skills

LEARNING OUTSIDE CLASS

1 **Work in small groups. Make a list of three ways you can learn English outside the class.**

2 **Read the text and tick the things you do.**

These students tell us how they learn English after class …

> **Lei:** I like films, so I watch films in English with *subtitles in my language. ☐
> **Sofia:** I practise English on the Internet. There are lots of sites to practise grammar and vocabulary. ☐

> **Mohammed:** I meet my friends at lunch and we practise speaking together in English. Sometimes our English teacher meets us too. ☐
> **Daniel:** I read books in English, easy books called 'readers' you can borrow from the library. ☐

3 **Choose one of the things from your list and the passage and try them for next week.**

4 **In the next class, tell the other students what you tried.**

(*Subtitles: the words from the film in your language on the screen)

Review **Units 1 and 2** **23**

Teamwork

VOCABULARY

ADJECTIVES TO DESCRIBE CHARACTER

1 Work in pairs. Look at the pictures and say which words describe the people.

> friendly   sad   happy   intelligent   nervous   warm

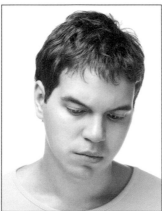

2 Complete the sentences with these words.

> shy   hardworking   talkative

1 A person who works hard is _____.

2 _____ people find it difficult to talk to other people.

3 When you are _____, you like to speak a lot.

Now match these words to their opposites 1–3.

> confident   lazy   quiet

3 Circle the correct adjectives to complete the text.

Student services

wAnted:

[1] *Intelligent / Lazy* students to join our [2] *shy / hardworking* team. We want students who can talk to people easily – are you [3] *quiet / confident*? Are you [4] *friendly / sad* with people? Help us research how first-year students feel.

Email: katrin@studentservices.gla.ac.uk

4 Work in pairs. Use the words in activities 1 and 2 to describe yourself.

> I'm a warm and friendly person but I'm not very hardworking.

5 Work in pairs. Do the Student services questionnaire. Then turn to page 125 to work out your score.

Student services

First-year student experience

New students often feel shy or nervous when they start university. We want to know how you feel. Please tick your answers, a, b or c.

1 What do you say when friends ask you to go somewhere with them?
  a I always say yes. ☐
  b I sometimes say yes. ☐
  c I usually say no. ☐

2 What do you do when someone starts a conversation with you?
  a I usually feel happy to talk. ☐
  b I try to finish the conversation quickly – I'm not usually very talkative. ☐
  c I often feel shy. ☐

3 Where do you usually like working or studying?
  a In a big group or class. ☐
  b In a small group. ☐
  c At my desk. ☐

4 How do other people describe you?
  a Talkative and confident. ☐
  b Warm and friendly. ☐
  c Thoughtful and quiet. ☐

5 What do you do when someone says something nice to you?
  a I usually feel good and smile. ☐
  b I say something nice to them. ☐
  c I feel nervous and think they want something. ☐

LISTENING

1 🔊 1.13 Listen to two students, Katrin and Li Bo, doing the questionnaire and circle their answers.

2 🔊 1.13 Listen again and choose the correct answers.

1 Katrin wants to find out …
  a who does well in their first year.
  b why Li Bo is busy.

2 Katrin thinks Li Bo … going out.
  a doesn't like
  b likes

3 Li Bo feels … working in big groups.
  a shy
  b confident

4 Li Bo feels happy when his … says his essay is good.
  a tutor
  b friend

GRAMMAR

ADVERBS OF FREQUENCY

You use adverbs of frequency to say how often you do something.

You often use adverbs of frequency to talk about routines.

Adverbs of frequency usually go before the main verb, but go after the verb *be*.

*I **sometimes** feel happy to talk.*
*He doesn't **always** say yes.*
*Where do you **usually** like working or studying?*
*I am **never** shy.*

 GRAMMAR REFERENCE PAGE 139

1 Look back at the Student services questionnaire on page 25. How many adverbs of frequency can you find?

2 Label the chart with the adverbs of frequency below.

often   sometimes   usually   never   always

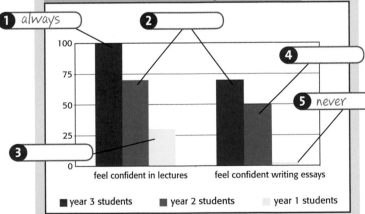

Results of student services questionnaire

1 always
2
3
4
5 never

100
75
50
25
0

feel confident in lectures   feel confident writing essays

■ year 3 students   ■ year 2 students   □ year 1 students

3 Put the underlined words in order.

1 Year 3 students <u>feel confident always</u> in lectures.
2 Year 2 students <u>confident are often</u> about their essays.
3 Students in year 1 <u>confident feel sometimes</u> in lectures.
4 My tutor <u>asks often us work to</u> in groups.
5 I <u>for never late am</u> class.

4 Make the sentences true for you using adverbs of frequency.

1 I ＿＿＿＿＿＿＿ enjoy meeting new people.
2 I ＿＿＿＿＿＿＿ like being alone.
3 I ＿＿＿＿＿＿＿ make plans for the weekend.
4 I ＿＿＿＿＿＿＿ stay at home and watch TV.

5 Write questions for the sentences in activity 4.

Do you enjoy meeting new people?

6 Walk around the class and find students with two answers the same as yours.

READING

1 Work in pairs. Look at the photographs and decide where each animal lives.

under the ground   in the air   on the ground

meerkat

snake

eagle

2 ⏱ (3min) **Read the passage in three minutes. Match the pictures in activity 1 with paragraphs A–C.**

Teamwork

A Meerkats live in the desert, with enemies everywhere. So how do they survive? They have all the skills to live there: they can hunt well, they can see their enemies from long distances. But they cannot survive alone. They survive because of one skill – they live and work together as a team. Meerkats are very good examples of the importance of teamwork. For them, teamwork is life or death.

B Meerkats live underground in large groups and have different group roles. Some watch for enemies, others look after the young meerkats and others go hunting. Meerkats can't talk like humans, but they can communicate with each other using different sounds. They can tell the others where the enemy is – an eagle in the air flying towards them or a snake on the ground.

C So what can people learn about teamwork from these amazing animals? They show us the importance of communication and making decisions. Teams are small groups of people who work together, but have different skills. Teams usually make better decisions than one person alone. Because the team often has people with different skills, it has more ideas than one person. With more ideas the group can choose the best answer to the problem.

D But teamwork isn't always the best way to make decisions – it has problems. It sometimes takes a long time and it usually needs good preparation. But because everyone in the team can help with making decisions, people usually work hard and feel good to be in a team.

3 **Read the passage again and match the ideas with the paragraphs. Underline the sentences that helped you find the idea in the paragraph.**

1 what is a team — Paragraph _____
2 the importance of teamwork — Paragraph _____
3 some difficulties with teamwork — Paragraph _____
4 working together and communicating — Paragraph _____

4 **Find words in the article which mean …**

1 s_____: to continue to live (paragraph A)
2 s_____: something you can do well (paragraph A)
3 r_____: what a person has when they are part of a team (paragraph B)
4 d_____: when you make a choice (paragraph C)
5 p_____: getting something ready, or getting yourself ready (paragraph D)

Bridge to IELTS

FINDING MAIN POINTS

Many IELTS reading questions ask you to understand the main points. Read all the passage quickly first, then read it again and underline the main points in each paragraph.

GRAMMAR

CAN / CAN'T FOR ABILITY

You use *can* to talk about the skills you have and what you are able to do.

Can is followed by a verb without *to* and is the same for all personal pronouns.

*With more ideas the group **can** choose the best answer to the problem.*

*But they **cannot** survive in the desert alone.*

*What **can** people learn about teamwork from these amazing animals?*

📖 **GRAMMAR REFERENCE PAGE 139**

1 Choose the correct words.

Meerkats …

1 *can / can't* see long distances.
2 *can / can't* hunt well.
3 *can / can't* survive alone.
4 *can / can't* talk like people.
5 *can / can't* communicate with each other.
6 *can / can't* see where an enemy is.

2 Complete the sentences with *can* or *can't*.

1 Sara is a good leader – she _____ always take difficult decisions.
2 I _____ understand why Lina is late. She knows when the meeting starts.
3 Can Winston speak French? Yes, he _____.
4 Good teams _____ do difficult things well.

3 Write *can* or *can't* to make the sentences true for you.

1 I _____ work in teams very well.
2 I _____ make good decisions by myself.
3 I _____ often understand other people's feelings.
4 I _____ always get what I want at work.

4 Work in pairs. Talk about your answers.

LISTENING

1 Work in pairs. Ask and answer the questions.

1 Are you good at interviews? Why / Why not?
2 How do people prepare for interviews?

2 Complete the job advert with these words.

experience   skills   qualifications

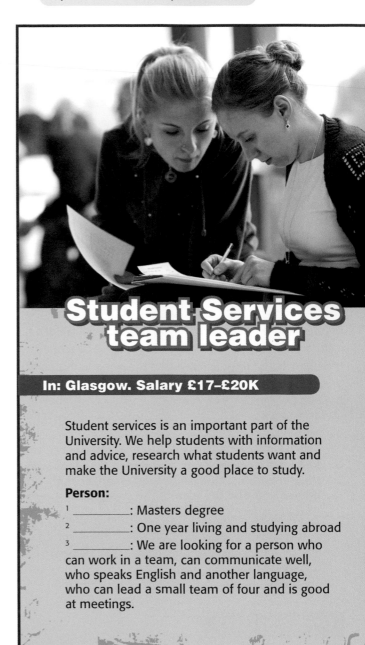

Student Services team leader

In: Glasgow. Salary £17–£20K

Student services is an important part of the University. We help students with information and advice, research what students want and make the University a good place to study.

Person:

¹ _____: Masters degree
² _____: One year living and studying abroad
³ _____: We are looking for a person who can work in a team, can communicate well, who speaks English and another language, who can lead a small team of four and is good at meetings.

PRONUNCIATION

STRONG AND WEAK FORMS: *CAN* AND *CAN'T*

1 🔊 **1.15** **Listen and write the number of each sentence next to the correct pronunciation of *can* or *can't*.**

/kən/ _____ _____ _____ _____

/kæn/ /kɑːnt/ _____ _____

2 🔊 **1.16** **Listen to the sentences. Tick when you hear the strong form of *can*.**

1 Can you work well under pressure? ☐
2 Yes, I can do that. ☐
3 I can speak English and Spanish. ☐
4 Yes, I can, too. ☐

3 🔊 **1.17** **Listen and answer the questions for you.**

Living IELTS

TALKING ABOUT ABILITY

1 🔊 **1.18** **Listen and practise the expressions.**

I'm very good at teamwork.
I'm quite good at teamwork.
I'm not bad at working under pressure.
I'm OK at working under pressure.
I can work well alone.
I can't work well in large groups.

2 **Work in pairs. Take turns to interview each other for the job in Listening activity 2.**

- Write a list of questions with *Can you ...? Are you good at ...?*
- Ask each other the questions.
- Try to give examples for each answer.

3 **Read the advert again and answer the questions.**

1 What is the job for?
2 Where is the job?
3 How many people are in the team?

4 🔊 **1.14** **Listen to Pilar being interviewed for the job in the advert in activity 2. Tick the things they talk about.**

1 working in a team ☐
2 good communication ☐
3 language skills ☐
4 experience abroad ☐
5 leading a team ☐

5 🔊 **1.14** **Listen again and choose T (true) or F (false).**

1 Pilar has a Masters of Science. T / F
2 Pilar can't speak German. T / F
3 She is good at working in teams. T / F
4 She thinks she can lead a team. T / F

SPEAKING

A PERSON YOU ADMIRE

1 Work in pairs. Match the words with the photos.

> actor   political leader   business leader
> sportsman / sportswoman

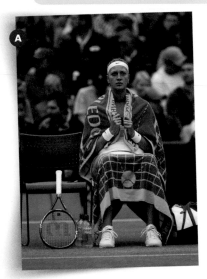

2 What do you know about the people in the photos? Use the words below.

> honest   intelligent   generous   kind
> funny   calm

3 Complete the text with some of the words in activity 2.

I really admire Leonardo DiCaprio. He's an actor, and he makes really good films. He's hardworking and ¹ _____ – he makes me laugh. I really admire him because he is ² _____ - he's rich and he his money to help people. He's also ³ _____; he has a website about the environment and he wants to change the world.

🔘 1.19 Listen to Drew talking to the IELTS examiner and check your answers.

4 🔘 1.20 Listen to Kavitha talking about a person she admires. Complete the table.

What is his / her name?	
What does he / she do?	
Why does Kavitha admire him / her?	

Bridge to IELTS

GIVING INFORMATION ABOUT PEOPLE AND THINGS

When you are giving information about people or things you can begin with *someone who is …* or *people who are …* for people and *something which … * for things.

5 Think of a famous person you admire. Make notes about them. Use the questions in activity 4.

6 Work in pairs. Take turns to talk about the topic card. Use the notes you made in activity 5 to help you.

Describe a famous person you admire.

You should say:
- who they are
- what they do
- what you admire about them
and explain the reasons you admire them.

WRITING

DESCRIBING A GOOD LEADER

1 **Work in pairs. Circle the ideas you agree with.**

A good leader …
1 **a** is confident.
   b is talkative.

2 **a** has a lot of experience.
   b has new ideas.

3 **a** is good at making decisions.
   b is good at communication.

4 **a** listens to people.
   b is an expert and doesn't listen to other people.

2 **Read a paragraph describing a good leader. Tick the ideas below it mentions.**

- ☐ the character of a good leader
- ☐ what the person is good at
- ☐ who the person is
- ☐ their home
- ☐ the person's relationship with the writer
- ☐ an example of good leadership

> My boss, Marianne, is a good leader and a person I really admire. She is a very honest person and she is usually calm and kind. She is also good at talking to people. She asks people what they think and listens to them too. She has lots of experience and can solve difficult problems.

WRITING SKILLS

LINKING IDEAS WITH *AND*, *TOO* AND *ALSO*

3 **Look at the paragraph in activity 2 again. Complete the sentences with these words.**

> and   too   also

1 _____ joins two ideas.
2 _____ and _____ add an idea.
3 You usually put _____ at the end of the sentence.
4 _____ usually comes after the verb.

4 **Complete the sentences with *and*, *too* and *also*.**

1 Peng is intelligent. She is hardworking _____.
2 Jacques is calm. He is _____ quiet.
3 Esra can make good decisions _____ she can communicate well.
4 A good leader asks questions. They _____ listen to the answers.
5 We enjoy working with our new manager. We can learn from him _____.

5 **Think of a person who is a good leader that you admire. Make notes about them. Think about …**

- the person's relationship with you (boss / sister / friend …).
- their character.
- what they are good at.
- an example of good leadership.

6 **Complete the text. Use the notes you made in activity 5.**

My [1] _____ is a person I really admire. He / She is a [2] _____ person and he / she is usually [3] _____ and [4] _____. He / She is also good at [5] _____. He / She has [6] _____ and can [7] _____ too.

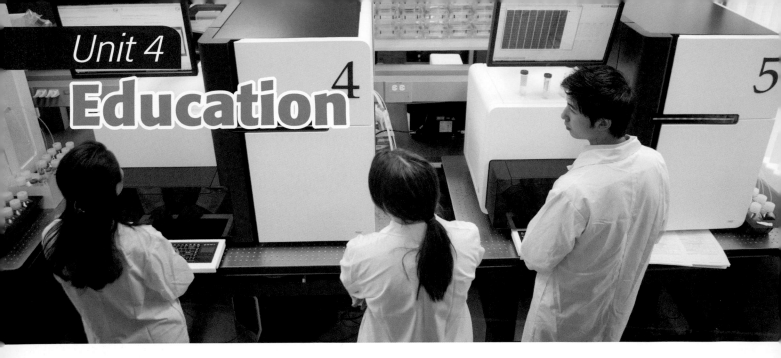

Education

VOCABULARY

ACADEMIC SUBJECTS AND HIGHER EDUCATION

1   **Match the words below with the pictures.**

  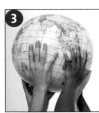

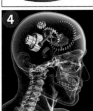  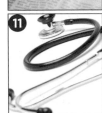

- ☐ geology
- ☐ literature
- ☐ maths
- ☐ computer science
- ☐ business
- ☐ law
- ☐ engineering
- ☐ medicine
- ☐ languages
- ☐ sociology
- ☐ psychology
- ☐ biology

2   **Work in pairs. Say what you know about the subjects in activity 1.**

3   **Complete the text with these words.**

> higher education   degree   qualification   pass

Students at college or university are in
[1] _____. When you take an exam and
are successful, you [2] _____ and get
a [3] _____. At university, this is called
a [4] _____.

PRONUNCIATION

SYLLABLE STRESS

1   🔊 1.21 **Listen and underline the stressed syllable in each word.**

geology	languages	psychology
literature	sociology	biology

2   🔊 1.21 **Listen again and repeat the words.**

READING

1   **Read the webpage and tick how you can win the competition.**

get good grades	☐
have lots of friends	☐
help other people	☐
speak English very well	☐

International Student in Canada Prize

Are you studying in Canada? Are you an international student? Then this competition is for you. Are you helping other people? Is life at university in Canada changing you? Enter the competition with a letter about your experiences. We are waiting to hear about your life in Canada. Write a letter about it – and you can win a prize of $3,000!

2 **Read the webpage again and complete the phrases with the verbs below.**

> enter   help   study   win   write

1 _____ a prize   4 _____ other people
2 _____ a competition 5 _____ a letter
3 _____ in a country

3 ⏱(3min) **Read the competition letters. Which student(s) is each sentence describing? Write Atakan, Karl or Valli.**

1 _____ has a job after class.
2 _____ is having a very good time.
3 _____ is helping people learn another language.
4 _____ and _____ are undergraduate students.

Email 🔍

1 My name's Atakan and I'm studying geology at the University of Calgary. I'm having a great time! Most evenings I party with friends – I listen to music and go dancing. I like to meet other people and practise my English. Because of my busy social life I'm not studying for my undergraduate degree very much. Am I enjoying myself? Yes, I am!

Email 🔍

2 I'm Karl and I'm an undergraduate student. I'm really enjoying my time here. I'm studying biology at Montreal University and working part time in a supermarket. I don't miss my home in Germany and I'm planning to stay in Canada. The way I see the world is changing because the other workers in the supermarket are helping me to understand Canadian society.

Email 🔍

3 My name's Valli, I'm at the University of Toronto and I'm a postgraduate student. My subject is languages and I'm doing very well. But my real education is after class – I'm teaching Arabic to young children in a local school. I'm helping my community and I'm learning about my subject.

4 **Read the letters again and choose the correct answers.**

1 Atakan … work.
   a does a lot of   **b** doesn't do much

2 Karl … to go back home to Germany.
   a wants   **b** doesn't want

3 Valli is learning about her subject by …
   a reading.   **b** teaching.

5 **Find words and phrases in the emails which mean …**

1 go out to meet people and dance (email 1)
   p_____
2 work for a few hours a day (email 2) p_____
   t_____
3 people living together in a country or city (email 2)
   s_____
4 people living together in a small area (email 3)
   c_____

6 **Match the student level, the degree and length of course.**

1	undergraduate	A	masters degree	i	three years
2	postgraduate	B	bachelors degree	ii	one year

GRAMMAR

PRESENT CONTINUOUS

You use the present continuous to talk about actions happening now.

You often use it with phrases and words like *at the moment* and *now*.

You form the present continuous with *be* + verb + *-ing*.

I'm teaching Arabic to young children.
I'm not studying very hard.
Am I enjoying myself? Yes, *I am.* / No, *I'm not.*

📖 **GRAMMAR REFERENCE PAGE 139**

1 **Look back at the emails in Reading and underline examples of the present continuous.**

2 **Complete Frederika's letter with the present continuous form of the verbs in brackets.**

Hi, I'm Frederika and I ¹ _____ (study) design engineering at Université Laval. The course I ² _____ (take) is in English and French, so my languages ³ _____ (get) better at the same time. At the moment we ⁴ _____ (work) on our final project. We're working day and night so we ⁵ _____ (not sleep) very much. At the end of the course, I ⁶ _____ (hope) to work in New York.

3 **Write questions in the present continuous.**

1 What / you / study ?
2 Which part of the course / you / enjoy ?
3 What / work on / at the moment ?
4 What / you / hope to do after the course ?

4 **Work in pairs. Ask and answer the questions in activity 3.**

Discussion

Work in groups. Decide which student in activity 3 on page 33 to give the *International Student in Canada Prize* to and why.

READING

1 **Work in pairs. Ask and answer the questions.**

1 Do you know anyone studying abroad?
2 Who are they?
3 Where are they?
4 What are they studying?

2 ⏱(3min) **Read the passage on page 35 in three minutes and answer the questions.**

1 How many international students are there in the world?
2 How many international students are there in China?
3 How many international campuses are there in the world?
4 How many countries are mentioned in the passage?

Bridge to IELTS

SCANNING A READING PASSAGE

Looking quickly through the passage for numbers and names can start to help you understand the general meaning of the passage.

3 **Read the text again and choose the correct answer, a or b.**

1 There are … of choices in education for students today.
   a a lot
   b not a lot

2 Students are looking for universities …
   a in English-speaking countries only.
   b with an interesting social life.

3 Some students …
   a go to work overseas.
   b think Western-style education is bad.

4 International students bring home … ideas.
   a business
   b up-to-date

5 Universities are changing because …
   a of international education.
   b they are exciting places.

Home or away?

Choices in today's education

A Students today have many educational choices and some students are leaving their country to study. There are four million international students and this is increasing every year.

B Of course, lots of international students travel to America, Canada, Britain and Australia. But students aren't just going to English-speaking countries – more than 200 000 international students are studying in China today. In Europe, the number of international students is going up too. They are looking for good universities with an interesting social life.

C Students can also get an international education in their home country. There are over 160 international campuses all over the world and this number is growing. Students at these campuses have a Western-style education. Some people think this is a bad thing because the students often leave their home countries and go overseas to work.

D Other people say there are lots of advantages to an international education. International students leave universities with up-to-date ideas and take this knowledge back to their countries. Students also learn the language and culture of these countries. They learn about work, business and how to do well in the global economy.

E International education is changing universities too. Now they are becoming exciting places, with students from all over the world. International students bring new ideas and new ways of looking at the world.

4 Find these words in the text and match them with the definitions.

Western   campus   global   overseas

1 _____: the buildings of a university or college
2 _____: something from America or Europe
3 _____: a country far away from yours
4 _____: about the whole world

GRAMMAR

PRESENT CONTINUOUS AND PRESENT SIMPLE

1 Read the grammar explanations a) and b). Match sentences 1–4 to each one.

a) You use the present simple to talk about habits and things which are generally true.

b) You use the present continuous to talk about things which are happening now or changing.

1 Some students are leaving their country to study. ___

2 International students leave universities with up-to-date ideas. ___

3 Now they are becoming exciting places. ___

4 They learn about work, business and how to do well in the global economy. ___

📖 **GRAMMAR REFERENCE PAGE 139**

2 Complete the sentences with the present simple or present continuous form of the verbs in brackets.

1 It _____ (be) important to have a good education.

2 The number of international students in China _____ (go up).

3 Going to university _____ (cost) a lot of money.

4 Please be quiet, the students _____ (do) a test.

5 I can't help you now because I _____ (eat) my dinner.

3 Complete the sentences so they are true for your country. Use the present continuous form of the verbs below.

go up   go down   grow   stay the same

1 The cost of education _____.

2 The number of women in education _____.

3 The importance of English in education _____.

4 The choice of subjects at university _____.

Discussion

Work in pairs. Say how education is changing in your country. Use the sentences you completed in activity 3.

LISTENING

1 Work in pairs and guess if these statements are true or false.

1 In Britain, more women than men are in higher education. ___

2 More men finish university than women. ___

3 More women than men take science subjects. ___

4 The trends in British universities are similar to those in other countries. ___

2 💿 1.22 Listen to Esra talking about changes in education. Check your guesses in activity 1.

3 💿 1.22 Listen again and complete the chart.

	women %	men %
studying in higher education	1 _____	37.2
getting a good degree	2 _____	60
studying computer science	19.4	3 _____
studying engineering	4 _____	86

PRONUNCIATION

NUMBERS

1 💿 1.23 Listen and circle the numbers you hear, a or b.

1 **a** 39   **b** 39.9
2 **a** 18.1   **b** 80.1
3 **a** 12%   **b** 2%

2 💿 1.24 Listen and practise saying the numbers.

Discussion

1 Walk around the class. Ask other students which of these subjects they are interested in and note their answers.

name	maths	computer science	engineering	business	medicine	other
Rafik		✓		✓		

2 Complete the sentences using the information about the other students.

1 _____ (number) students in the class are interested in _____. (subject)
2 _____ % of students are interested in _____.
3 Not many students like _____.
4 More students are interested in _____ than _____.

3 Share your information with the class.

SPEAKING

MY STUDIES

1 Work in pairs. Look at the picture and say which subject you think they are studying.

2 [1.25] Listen to three students and tick the things they speak about.

1 The place they are studying. ☐
2 The subject they are studying. ☐
3 Where they live. ☐
4 The cost of the course. ☐
5 What their subject is about. ☐
6 Why they are interested in the subject. ☐

3 [1.25] Listen again and choose the correct answers.

1 Adel is studying …
  a geology.   **b** biology.

2 He wants to understand …
  a how plants grow. **b** how life started.

3 Yun is studying …
  a sociology.   **b** languages.

4 Society in China is changing …
  a fast.   **b** slowly.

5 Esra is in …
  a Oman.   **b** Scotland.

6 She is studying the differences between …
  a boys and girls.   **b** men and women.

Living IELTS

TALKING ABOUT YOUR STUDIES

[1.26] Listen and practise the expressions.

place:
It's a good place to learn.
It's a great place to study.
subject:
I'm studying biology.
My subject is sociology.
interest:
I'm interested in biology.
I find it fascinating.

4 Think of a subject you are studying. Make notes. Think about …

- where you are learning.
- what you study in your subject.
- why you think it is interesting.

5 Work in pairs. Take turns to talk about the topic card. Use the notes you made in activity 4 to help you.

Describe your education.

You should talk about:
- where you are studying
- what subject you are studying
- what the subject is about
and why you are interested in it.

WRITING

DESCRIBING GRAPHS AND TRENDS

1 Match the charts with the words below.

bar chart   line graph   pie chart

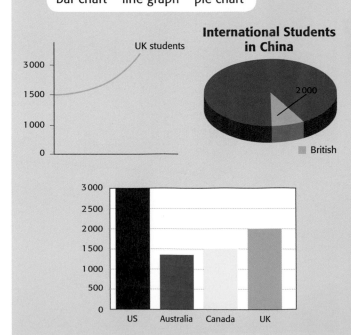

2 Put the words below into the correct group.

> going down   increasing   staying the same
> decreasing   growing   falling   rising   going up

A getting bigger: _____ _____ _____ _____
B getting smaller: _____ _____ _____
C no movement: _____

3 Read the text and choose which chart in activity 1 it is describing.

The line graph shows the number of students from Britain studying in China. On the left, we can see the number of students in thousands and on the right we can see the time in years. The number of students is increasing. It is growing to 2,000 students this year. This shows that more students see China as a good place to study.

WRITING SKILLS
PHRASES TO DESCRIBE TRENDS

4 Read the text again and number the questions in the order the information is given in the text.

a What is happening? ☐
b What information is in the chart? ☐
c What does the chart show? ☐
d Why it is happening? ☐

Bridge to IELTS

STRUCTURING INFORMATION ABOUT A CHART

Task 1 of the written paper often asks you to write about a chart or graph. You can use the questions in activity 4 to help you give the information in the correct order.

5 Look at the graph and complete the text. Use the words and phrases below.

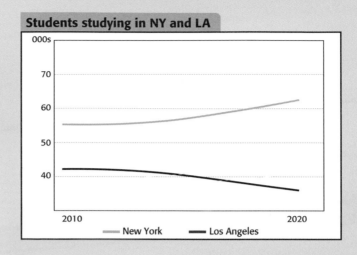

Students studying in NY and LA

New York   Los Angeles

> is becoming   line graph   On the
> left   number of   is decreasing

The ¹ _____ shows the number of international students in two American cities.
² _____, we can see the number of students and on the right we can see the time in years. The ³ _____ students is increasing in New York to around 60000. In Los Angeles, the number of students ⁴ _____. This shows that New York ⁵ _____ a popular city for international students.

6 Look at the graph and complete the text.

Students studying languages in Canada

French   German   Arabic

The ¹ _____ shows the number of students in Canada studying ² _____. On the left, we can see the ³ _____ and at the bottom we can see the ⁴ _____. The number of students studying French ⁵ _____ from around 5250 to ⁶ _____. The number of students studying German ⁷ _____. The number of students studying Arabic ⁸ _____. This shows that ⁹ _____ a popular language for Canadian students.

Review Units 3 and 4

GRAMMAR AND VOCABULARY

1 Write questions with *Can*.

1 / you speak two languages
  <u>Can you speak two languages?</u>
2 / you remember vocabulary easily
3 / you do maths well
4 / you work well in teams
5 (your question) _____

2 Walk round the class and find out how many people can do 1–5. Write down the answers.

3 Write sentences about the answers in activity 2.

4 Find the mistakes in the sentences.

1 Lydia cans speak four languages.
2 You don't can study in an Australian University with an IELTS score of 3.
3 Pablo no can do maths.
4 You can play the piano?

5 Read the passage and choose the correct words to complete the sentences.

Elspeth is a researcher at a University. She has a lot of things to do and works every weekend and every evening. She [1] *always / sometimes* works hard. She [2] *never / often* reads a lot of articles; she reads three or four every week. Elspeth is researching what people think about education. Every month Elspeth talks to people about it, she [3] *sometimes / always* interviews people for her research. She [4] *always / often* likes meeting her research team – she enjoys it every time they meet.

6 Complete the sentences with the present simple or present continuous form of the verbs below.

do	grow	drink	study	learn

1 These plants grow in hot countries. But in our biology labs now we _____ two of these plants.
2 Ali, what _____ you _____ now? I want to talk to you.
3 In engineering we _____ a lot about buildings.
4 Please be quiet. I _____ for a test tomorrow.
5 Would you like some coffee? No, thanks. I don't _____ coffee.

7 Complete the text with the correct form of the verbs in brackets.

Cecil [1] _____ (work) in a bank every day. He works as a bank clerk but now he [2] _____ (study) for a Masters in Business. At the moment he [3] _____ (learn) about working with people and he [4] _____ (write) an essay about teamwork. Cecil is studying because he [5] _____ (want) to get a better job.

VOCABULARY

1 Put the words into groups.

talkative	honest	quiet	nervous
sad	generous	shy	lazy	kind

A positive: _____ _____ _____
B not positive and not negative: _____
  _____ _____
C negative: _____ _____ _____

2 Complete the definitions with six words from activity 1.

1 Someone is _____ when they don't like talking to people.
2 A _____ person likes speaking to people.
3 A _____ person doesn't like work.
4 Someone who tells the truth is _____.
5 A _____ person helps people by giving them money or presents.
6 When someone helps other people, they are _____.

3 Complete the course catalogue with these words.

business   literature   computer science
engineering   biology

1 _____ : This course includes plays and poems by famous writers.

2 _____ : On this course you study how PCs work.

3 _____ : In this subject, students study living things.

4 _____ : Students learn how buildings, bridges and towers work.

5 _____ : This course is about companies and management.

4 Match the words with the definitions.

interview   experience   skills   qualifications

1 Meeting someone to talk to them to get a job. _____

2 The things that happen in your life. _____
3 What you can or can't do. _____
4 You get these when you pass a test at the end of school or university. _____

Bridge to IELTS

LISTENING TEST PREPARATION

1 Read the text and choose the correct answers.

1 The listening test takes
   a) *30*   **b)** *40*   **c)** *50* minutes in total.
2 The first listening passages are about
   a) *general academic*   **b)** *academic* subjects.

Listening test

The listening test has four parts and lasts 50 minutes. You have 40 minutes to listen and write your answers on the question paper then 10 minutes to copy your answers onto the answer sheet. The first part is often two or more people speaking about general academic subjects. The second part has one person talking. The next parts are more formal and academic. Studying *Bridge to IELTS* helps you to practise all parts of the listening test.

2 Work in pairs. Think of three ways you can practise your listening skills outside the class.

Study Skills

THINKING ABOUT YOUR STUDY HABITS

1 Work in pairs. List six good study habits.

2 Read the passage and check your answers.

Good students usually have good study habits. They often plan their learning – where, when and how often they are studying. Think about where and how you study best – in your own room, in a library, at school? Planning a study schedule is important – do a little bit often and regularly. Students often forget what they learn, so it's important to revise. Before your class, look at the notes from the last lesson. At the end of the week check your notes and test yourself.

3 Read the study habits and tick the ones for you.

1 In English, I'm good at ...
   - working in pairs. ☐
   - working in groups. ☐
   - correcting myself. ☐
   - correcting other students. ☐
2 I can ...
   - manage my time well. ☐
   - find ways to practise English outside class. ☐
3 I always / usually / often / sometimes / never ...
   - study in the same place. ☐
   - write down new words. ☐
   - study in a quiet place. ☐
   - use a monolingual dictionary. ☐
   - practise English with my friends. ☐

4 Decide three things in activity 3 you would like to practise. In the next class tell the other students about how well you did them.

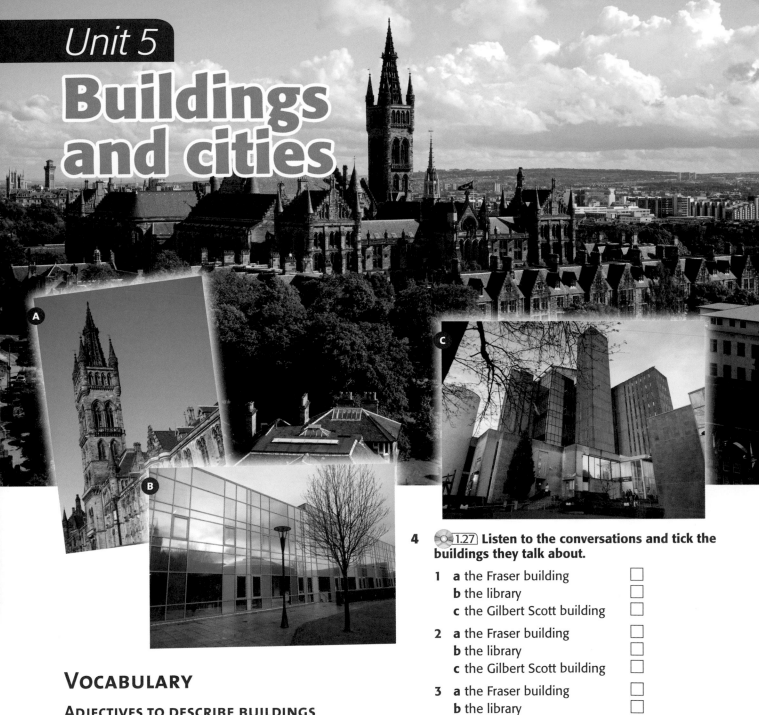

Unit 5
Buildings and cities

VOCABULARY

ADJECTIVES TO DESCRIBE BUILDINGS

1 Work in pairs. Describe the buildings. Use the words below.

> old huge stone glass ugly unusual modern fantastic concrete tall small brick wonderful

2 Put the adjectives in activity 1 in four groups: *size*, *age*, *material* and *opinion*.

3 Work in pairs. Ask and answer the questions.

1 What do you think of the buildings in the pictures?
2 Which buildings do you like? Which do you dislike? Why?

4 🔊 1.27 **Listen to the conversations and tick the buildings they talk about.**

1 **a** the Fraser building ☐
  b the library ☐
  c the Gilbert Scott building ☐

2 **a** the Fraser building ☐
  b the library ☐
  c the Gilbert Scott building ☐

3 **a** the Fraser building ☐
  b the library ☐
  c the Gilbert Scott building ☐

5 🔊 1.27 **Listen again and choose the correct answers.**

Conversation 1

1 The person is looking for …
  a the School of Engineering.
  b the Business School.
  c the English as a Foreign Language department.

Conversation 2

2 The person wants to find a place to …
  a rest. **b** read. **c** eat.

Conversation 3

3 The library is made of …
  a glass. **b** brick. **c** concrete.

LISTENING

1 Work in pairs. Look at the pictures and say what you think the object is.

A

B

C

2 Match the words with the definitions.

1	rod	a	a place for keeping money or other things safe
2	seed	b	a long thin shape
3	bank	c	how we can see in the daytime
4	sunlight	d	what a plant grows from

3 🔊 1.28 Listen and number the pictures in the order they are mentioned.

4 🔊 1.28 Listen again and complete the text with one word or a number for each gap.

The Seed Cathedral was the UK exhibition [1] _____ at the World Fair in Shanghai. There were many rods on the building. There were [2] _____ at the ends of each one. There was a [3] _____ inside each rod which came on at night. The idea was that [4] _____ can make cities good places to live in. The theme of the World Fair was 'Better [5] _____, better life'. After the World Fair was over, they decided to give the rods to [6] _____ in the UK and China.

5 Choose Y (yes) or N (no).

1	Was the Shanghai World Fair in 2011?	Y / N
2	Were there many visitors to the building?	Y / N
3	Were the lights inside each rod very small?	Y / N
4	Was there a lot of technology in the building?	Y / N
5	Was there a lot of noise inside the building?	Y / N
6	Was the building popular with visitors?	Y / N

6 Underline the correct information.

1 The Seed Cathedral was in Shanghai for **six months / a year**.
2 The rods were **clear / black** in colour.
3 There were **six thousand / sixty thousand** rods in total.
4 Professor Gu was at the building **a few / many times**.

GRAMMAR

PAST SIMPLE OF BE

was = the past tense of *am* and *is*; *were* = the past tense of *are*

It **was** a fantastic building. It **wasn't** here for a very long time.
There **were** seeds on the end of each rod. They **weren't** very big.
Was there any special reason for the design? Yes, there **was**. / No, there **wasn't**.
Were the rods black? Yes, they **were**. / No, they **weren't**.

📖 *GRAMMAR REFERENCE PAGE 140*

1 Choose the correct answers.

1 I *was / were* at work on Friday.
2 We *was / were* late home last night.
3 He *wasn't / weren't* late for the meeting.
4 There was a lot of rain so the roads *was / were* very wet.
5 They *wasn't / weren't* at home when I called.
6 It *was / were* cold yesterday.

2 Complete the sentences with *was, wasn't, were* or *weren't*.

1 The Seed Cathedral _____ (not) here for very long.
2 Visitors from many countries _____ at the World Fair.
3 There _____ (not) hundreds of rods – there were thousands!
4 The seeds _____ from all over the world.
5 It _____ very quiet and peaceful inside the building.
6 The building _____ a great success. People loved it!

3 Put the words in order to make questions.

1 at / home / you / Were / yesterday ?
2 she / Was / weekend / with / you / last ?
3 in / they / a / car / Were / blue ?
4 a / party / it / Was / big ?
5 the / he / Was / at / World / Fair ?

Discussion

Work in pairs. Say what you like or dislike about the Seed Cathedral and why.

READING

1 Work in pairs and do the quiz. Guess the answers.

World Fairs

Where can you see the whole world in one place? At a World Fair! World Fairs take place every two or three years in different countries. See how much you know about them.

1 The first World Fair was in …
  a Shanghai.
  b London.

2 World Fairs are …
  a very big markets.
  b special buildings from different countries.

3 The Eiffel Tower was …
  a an entrance to the Paris World Fair.
  b nothing to do with the World Fair.

2 Read the passage and check your answers to the quiz questions.

THE EIFFEL TOWER

A World Fairs are great adverts for countries. They show the world your national culture and advertise your country. World Fairs started in London in 1851 and celebrated industrial technology and design. Other countries also wanted to hold World Fairs. Now the event goes to a different country every few years – in 2010 it was in Shanghai in China, then in 2015, it will be Turin, in Italy.

B The Eiffel Tower in Paris was the entrance to the 1889 World Fair. The French engineer Gustave Eiffel designed the tower. He wanted to show that iron could be as strong as stone, and could also be much higher. Construction of the tower started in 1887. 132 workers and 50 engineers completed it in two years and a team of twenty five painters used brushes to paint it. They needed approximately 60 tons of paint!

3 Read the passage again and match ideas 1–4 with paragraphs A–D.

1 why World Fairs remain important today   A
2 when and why World Fairs began   B
3 how they constructed the tower   C
4 how people reacted to the design of the tower   D

4 Complete the sentences with the words from the text.

1 a_____: information that tries to encourage people to buy things (Paragraph A)
2 e_____: the door, gate or opening where you go into a place (Paragraph B)
3 s_____: a building or large landmark (Paragraph C)
4 l_____: something such as a famous building that helps you know where you are in a place (Paragraph D)

Discussion

Work in pairs. Discuss the questions.

1 Would you like to visit a World Fair? Why / Why not?
2 Which World Fair city mentioned in the text would you most like to visit? Why?

Many people didn't like the tower at first.

C Many people didn't like the tower at first. They believed it was too tall for the city. They called it a 'street lamp' and 'candlestick'. The writer Guy de Maupassant hated it, but enjoyed lunch in the tower's restaurant every day. He explained that it was the one place in Paris where he didn't see the structure! The organisers of the World Fair wanted to take down the tower after the event. They planned to sell the metal, but in the end this didn't happen. The government decided the tower was important for communication.

D World Fairs leave important buildings after them. Today the Eiffel Tower is a famous landmark of the city of Paris. Around six million tourists visit it each year. The first World Fair had a big impact on society, education, international business and the tourist trade. This is still true today.

GRAMMAR

PAST SIMPLE: REGULAR VERBS

You use the past simple to talk about actions and events that have finished.

You form regular past tense forms by adding *-ed* to the verb. The form is the same for all personal pronouns.

*Gustave Eiffel **designed** the tower.*

You form negatives with the auxiliary verb *did / didn't* and the infinitive form of the verb.

*Guy de Maupassant **didn't like** the tower.*

 GRAMMAR REFERENCE PAGE 140

1 Write the past tense forms of the verbs in the box. Use the passage on page 45 to help you.

> believe   call   design   enjoy
> hate   need   plan   decide

2 Complete the sentences with the past simple form of the verbs in brackets.

1 Building workers and engineers _____ (use) iron to build the tower.
2 Gustave Eiffel _____ (start) work on the design of the tower in 1887.
3 The construction workers _____ (complete) the tower in two years.
4 Many people hated the tower at first, but a few people _____ (like) it.
5 I'm glad the government _____ (decide) to keep the tower. I think it's amazing!

3 Choose the correct answers.

1 They *enjoyed / didn't enjoy* the museum but they didn't like the art gallery.
2 He *called / didn't call* her during his trip. He phoned her before he travelled.
3 I *used / didn't use* the underground in Paris. I wanted to see the city on foot.
4 We *celebrated / didn't celebrate* my birthday in Paris. We really enjoyed our time there.
5 She *needed / didn't need* to pay to visit the tower. It was very expensive!
6 I *hated / didn't hate* my visit to the tower. I really liked it!

4 Complete the sentences with the negative form of the verbs in brackets.

1 They _____ (want) to keep the tower after the World Fair.
2 She _____ (enjoy) her visit to the tower.
3 We _____ (travel) around the city by car.
4 I _____ (plan) to go the tower, but I was really glad I visited it.
5 Guy de Maupassant _____ (design) the tower.

5 Complete the sentences for you. Then work in pairs and compare your sentences.

1 Last weekend I enjoyed _____

2 Yesterday I visited _____

3 Last year I wanted to _____

4 A few days ago I decided to _____

6 Match the beginnings 1–5 with the endings a–e to make sentences.

1 The name of the building is
2 It is in
3 They started to build it
4 They used
5 They completed it

a in 1887.
b the Eiffel Tower.
c in two years.
d iron to build it.
e Paris.

7 Work in pairs. Student A, turn to page 124. Student B, turn to page 126. Read the information. Then tell your partner about these buildings.

PRONUNCIATION

-ed ENDING OF REGULAR VERBS

1 🎧 1.29 **Listen to the three ways of pronouncing the -ed ending of regular verbs. Match the words with the endings.**

1	started	/t/
2	designed	/ɪd/
3	liked	/d/

2 🎧 1.30 **Listen to the past tense verbs and put them in the table.**

/d/	/t/	/ɪd/
designed	liked	started

3 **Practise saying the words.**

Student A

Bridge to IELTS

USING A DICTIONARY

A good learner's dictionary provides a lot of important information about a word. This usually includes an example of the word, the type of word it is, for example: verb, noun, adjective, etc. It also includes the spelling, meaning, pronunciation, and an example of the word in a sentence.

Look at the dictionary entry for 'design' below. Match the part of the definition, 1–5, with the type of information it gives, a–e.

> ¹ **Design** ² /dɪˈzaɪn/ ³ verb ⁴ to decide how to make something, how it will look or how it will work. ⁵ *Jonathan Ive designed the iMac, the iPod and the iPad.*

1	_____	a	an example in a sentence
2	_____	b	the pronunciation of the word
3	_____	c	the type of word it is
4	_____	d	the spelling of the word
5	_____	e	the definition of the word

Student B

SPEAKING

A SPECIAL BUILDING

1 **Work in pairs. Ask and answer the questions.**

1 Are there any special buildings in your country? If so, where are they?
2 What do people think about them?
3 Do you think it is important to protect special buildings? Why? / Why not?

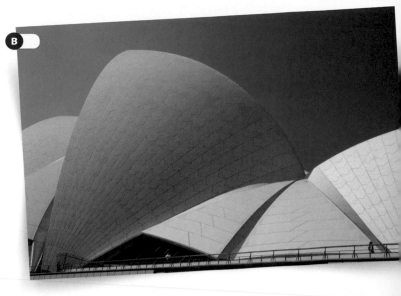

2 🔊 **1.31** **Listen to Kinga talking about the Sydney Opera House in Australia. Number the pictures in the order she talks about them. There is one picture she doesn't mention.**

3 🔊 **1.31** **Listen again and choose the correct answers.**

1 The designer was from *Denmark / Australia*.
2 The plans for the building changed *once / several times*.
3 The building attracts *very few / many* visitors.
4 Kinga particularly likes the *shape / size* of it.

Living IELTS

BEING POSITIVE

🔊 **1.32** **Listen and practise the expressions.**

It's a really spectacular building …
It's amazing in daylight …
It looks very dramatic at night …
It's definitely my favourite building …

4 **Think of a special building. Make notes about it. Think about …**

- what it is.
- what you know about it.
- where it is.
- why it is special for you.

Bridge to IELTS

WHEN YOU DON'T KNOW A WORD

You can give an example of a word if you are not sure of the word in English. You can use phrases like *It's similar to* … or *It's like* …. This will show the examiner that you are keen to express your ideas and get your point across.

5 **Work in pairs. Take turns to talk about the topic card. Use the notes you made in activity 4 to help you.**

Describe a special building.

You should say:
- what it is
- where it is
- Say what you know about it
and explain why it is special for you.

WRITING

DESCRIBING A CITY

1 Work in pairs. Match the two cities in the photographs with the fact files.

1

European Capital of Culture, 2008

Description	historical, lively
Size	medium-sized: population less than half a million
Location	north-west of UK, on the River Mersey, port
Industries	shipping, tourism

2

American Capital of Culture, 2004

Description	modern, exciting
Size	large: population 6 million
Location	South America, central Chile, capital city
Industries	finance, mining

2 Find words in the fact files which mean …

1 in the middle of a country or city c_____
2 a city near the sea p_____
3 the most important city in a country c_____
4 not big and not small m_____ - s_____
5 the people in a country p_____

WRITING SKILLS

ORGANISING A PARAGRAPH (1)

3 Read the description of Liverpool and number the ideas in the order they are mentioned in the text.

_____ the size of the city
_____ the name of the city and its main characteristics
_____ the main industries
_____ the location of the city
_____ when the city was a Capital of Culture

> Liverpool is a historical and lively city. The city is on the River Mersey, in the north-west of the UK. It is a medium-sized city with a population of less than half a million.
> Liverpool is a port and its main industries are shipping and tourism. In 2008, Liverpool was a European Capital of Culture – it was an important year in the city's history.

4 Look at the fact file about Santiago in activity 1 and complete the text. Order the information in the same order as in the text in activity 3.

Santiago is a [1] _____ and _____ city. The city is [2] _____. It is a [3] _____ city with a [4] _____. Santiago is the [5] _____ of Chile and its [6] _____. In [7] _____ – it was an important year in the city's history.

Liverpool

Santiago

Unit 6
Work

Vocabulary

Work

1 **Match the verbs 1–6 with the words a–f to make phrases.**

1	work as	**a**	a job
2	work	**b**	a new skill
3	apply for	**c**	experience
4	get	**d**	a volunteer
5	earn	**e**	full time
6	develop	**f**	good money

2 **Complete the definitions with the phrases in activity 1.**

1 _____: to work five days a week and eight hours a day

2 _____: to work because you want to and without being paid to do it

3 _____: to get knowledge from doing something

4 _____: to get well paid for the work you do

5 _____: to learn things you need to do a job well

6 _____: to ask for a job in a formal way

3 **Choose the correct answers.**

1 She *applied for the job / worked full time* and got it!

2 We *got experience / were well paid* when we worked as volunteers last summer.

3 I wanted to *develop new skills / work as a volunteer* in my full-time job but I didn't learn anything!

4 He didn't *work full time / apply for a job* last year – he only worked a few hours a week.

5 You don't get money if you *work as a volunteer / work full time* but it's good fun.

Reading

1 **Work in pairs. Ask and answer the questions.**

1 When was the last time you helped someone?

2 Who did you help?

3 Why did you help them?

4 How did you feel?

2 **Work in pairs. Look at the pictures and guess the answers. Choose three things.**

Volunteers at the Student Welcome Centre …
A give information to new students.
B get well paid.
C have qualifications.
D are friendly.
E work full time.
F can learn new skills.

3 **Read the text and check your guesses in activity 2.**

4 **Work in pairs. Discuss the question.**

Would you like to work as a volunteer in the Student Welcome Centre? Why? / Why not?

LISTENING

1 🔊 1.33 **Listen to two friends, Monika and Sebastien, talking about the Student Welcome Centre. Choose the correct answers.**

1 Where did Sebastien see an advertisement for volunteers?
   a in the Students Union
   b in the Student Welcome Centre
   c on the university website

2 When did Sebastien and Monika first meet?
   a last week
   b one year ago
   c two years ago

3 How did Monika feel when she first came?
   a excited
   b happy
   c lonely

4 Why did she choose to become a volunteer?
   a to improve her English
   b to get some work experience
   c to do something different

2 🔊 1.33 **Listen again and choose Y (yes) or N (no).**

1 Did they spend two hours in the queue
   on the first day of term?   Y / N
2 Did they speak about their families when
   they first met?   Y / N
3 Did Sebastien find it difficult to ask for
   help when he first arrived?   Y / N
4 Did they think the volunteers were
   friendly?   Y / N

Search ▶

Volunteer in the
Student Welcome Centre!

• Do you like helping people?
• Are you confident and friendly?
• Are you hardworking?
• Can you spare a few hours every week?

Did you answer 'yes' to these questions? Then read on!

Each term, we need student volunteers to work in the Student Welcome Centre. Volunteers help us give information and advice to new students about university life. You don't get paid to volunteer but you don't need any qualifications. You can develop skills, get work experience and make friends too. Do you want to share your own experience of campus life with new students from all over the world? Then apply online now!

GRAMMAR

PAST SIMPLE QUESTIONS

We form questions in the past simple with the auxiliary *did* + the infinitive form of the verb.

*Why **did** she **choose** to become a volunteer?*
***Did** they **think** the volunteers were unfriendly?*
*Yes, they **did**. / No, they **didn't**.*

📖 **GRAMMAR REFERENCE PAGE 140**

1 Put the words in order to make questions.

1 when / arrived / excited / feel / did / you / you ?
2 we / families / talk / about / our / did ?
3 he / volunteers / unfriendly / were / think / did / the ?
4 they / the / did / volunteers / ask / money / for ?
5 advertisement / she / see / the / did ?

2 Match the questions in activity 1 with the short answers.

1 No, she didn't.   4 Yes, I did.
2 No, he didn't.   5 Yes, we did.
3 No, they didn't.

3 Choose the correct word or phrase.

1 *What / Where* kind of job did you want when you were a child?
2 *Why / What time* did you decide to learn English?
3 *When / How much* did you last use your mobile phone?
4 *How much / When* did you last talk to your friend?
5 *What / Where* did you go on holiday last year?

4 Answer the questions in activity 3 for you. Then work in pairs and compare your answers.

5 Put the words in order to make questions about a job.

1 was / what / job / your ?
2 you / did / work / where ?
3 did / you / when / work ?
4 long / how / you / work / did ?
5 you / do / what / did ?

6 Work in pairs. Student A, turn to page 124. Student B, turn to page 126. Read the information. Then ask and answer the questions in activity 5 about the jobs.

READING

1 ⏱(3min) **Read the passage in three minutes and number the photographs in the order they are mentioned in the text.**

2 Read the text again. Put J for Jun or E for Eva.

1 _____ worked one day a week only.
2 _____ made some friends.
3 _____ wrote to an employer to ask for work.
4 _____ didn't want to work in a restaurant.
5 _____ worked full time.
6 _____ needed to earn money.

3 Read the text again. Choose T (true) or F (false).

1 Jun got a job in a cafe.   T / F
2 He enjoyed meeting different people.   T / F
3 Eva found a job in a museum.   T / F
4 Both Jun and Eva learnt very little in their jobs.   T / F

4 Find words in the text which mean …

1 b_____ - advantages or useful effects of doing something (paragraph A)
2 c_____ - making you try hard and put in a lot of effort (paragraph A)
3 p_____ - completely good (paragraph B)
4 v_____ - very useful (paragraph B)
5 r_____ - making you happy because you think it is important (paragraph B)

I need a job!

A University is a time for studying and making friends. But life on campus can be very expensive so many students decide to get part-time jobs. Most jobs that students do are in the retail industry, in shops and department stores or the hospitality industry, in cafes, restaurants and bars. These jobs include shop assistant, bar tender, waiter/waitress, or cinema staff. During term time, most students work part time but in the holidays they can work full time. Jun from Thailand worked as a shop assistant last year. He said, 'I needed to work because I spent all my money in the first few weeks of term! I didn't want to work in a restaurant or café, so I found a job in a sports shop on Saturdays. It was great. The people I worked with were really helpful. There were other benefits too. It was really challenging, I learnt a lot, I had a really good time and I met lots of people. I even made some good friends.'

B There are lots of holiday jobs in the summer too. Many of them are in tourism. Eva, from the UK, got a full-time job at a museum. 'I'm studying history,' she said, 'and I'm really interested in the past so I wrote to the director of the museum and she offered me a job. It was perfect! I gave out information to visitors and told them about the exhibits.' And like Jun, Eva felt she learnt a lot about work. 'I didn't just earn some money. I got very valuable work experience. It was really rewarding. I'm glad I did it,' she added.

GRAMMAR

PAST SIMPLE: IRREGULAR VERBS

Many verbs have irregular past simple forms.

I **found** a job in a sports shop.

You need to learn the past tense forms of irregular verbs. They are all different.

There is a list of irregular verbs on page 144.

📖 **GRAMMAR REFERENCE PAGE 140**

1 Find the past tense forms of these verbs in the text.

> find   get   give   learn   make
> meet   do   spend   write

2 Look back at the text. Complete the sentences. Use the words below.

> infinitive   affirmative sentences
> preposition   auxiliary

1 We use the irregular past form only in _____.
2 We use the _____ of the main verb after *did* or *didn't*.
3 The word order for questions is _____ + subject + infinitive.
4 We don't use a _____ with *last* and *yesterday*.

3 Complete the sentences with the past simple form of the verbs in brackets.

1 She _____ (have) a part-time job last year.
2 I _____ (spend) a lot of time looking for a job.
3 We _____ (not feel) it was a good experience.
4 He _____ (learn) to speak French last summer.
5 I applied for the job but I _____ (not get) it.

4 Complete the sentences with the affirmative or negative past simple form of the verbs below.

> find   give   make   meet   tell

1 She _____ some interesting people when she worked in the café.
2 I'm sorry I _____ you about my new job. I completely forgot!
3 I _____ some good friends in that job. I'm still in touch with them.
4 He _____ it very easy to get a job. It took a very long time.
5 Working in the restaurant _____ me the chance to practise my English!

Discussion

Work in pairs. Would you like to do one or more of the jobs mentioned in the text? Why? / Why not?

LISTENING

1 Work in pairs. Look at the pictures. Ask and answer the questions.

1 Do many students in your country have part-time or summer jobs?
2 Where do they work?
3 Why do they work?
   - to get money
   - to have something to do
   - to get work experience
   - another reason

2 🎧 1.34 Listen to two friends, Hiromi and Jakub, talking about a summer job. Which job in the photos are they talking about?

3 🎧 1.34 Listen again and tick the things they talk about.

1 how much she was paid ☐
2 how many hours she worked ☐
3 who she worked with ☐
4 what she did in her job ☐
5 how she found the job ☐
6 what she thought of the experience ☐

Living IELTS

TALKING ABOUT FEELINGS

🎧 1.35 Listen and practise the phrases.

I felt very nervous.
I didn't feel confident.
It made me happy.

Work in pairs. Say how you felt about a job you did.

I felt nervous / sad / happy / confident about my first job.

4 Circle the correct answer, a, b or c.

1 Why did Hiromi take a job?
 a to help with her living costs
 b to have something to do
 c to get work experience

2 What did she like least about her job?
 a getting up early
 b making sandwiches
 c working full time

3 What was the best thing about the job?
 a She could eat lots of sandwiches.
 b She made a lot of money.
 c She spoke to lots of people.

Discussion

Work in pairs. Discuss the questions.

1 Would you like to do a job like Hiromi? Why / Why not?
2 Which area of work would you most like to work in—retail or hospitality? Why?

Speaking

A REWARDING EXPERIENCE

1 **Work in pairs. Look at the pictures and discuss the question.**

Which activity do you think you would find most rewarding?

2 🔘 1.36 **Listen to two speakers, Jing and Agnes and match them to the pictures in activity 1.**

Jing _____
Agnes _____

3 🔘 1.36 **Listen again. Put J for Jing or A for Agnes.**

_____ made new friends.
_____ had a lot of responsibility.
_____ felt that the experience was relevant to her course.
_____ met someone who became special in her life.

PLAYING FOR TIME

Repeat the words on the card or make questions.
What did I do?
How did I feel about it?
Why was it so rewarding?
This will give you time to think about what to say next.

4 **Think of a time when you did something rewarding. Make notes about it. Think about …**

- what you did.
- how you felt about it.
- why it was so rewarding.

5 **Work in pairs. Take turns to talk about the topic card. Use the notes you made in activity 4 to help you.**

Describe a time you did something rewarding.

You should say:
- what you did
- how you felt about the experience
and explain why it was so rewarding.

PRONUNCIATION

DIFFERENT PRONUNCIATIONS OF THE LETTER *e*

1 🔘 1.37 **Listen to the pronunciation of the words. Match the sounds in bold with the correct pronunciation.**

1	h**e**lp	**a**	/iː/
2	answ**e**r	**b**	/ə/
3	sl**ee**p	**c**	/e/

2 🔘 1.38 **Listen and put the words below into the table.**

speaker   picture   friendly   well paid   read
week   welcome   confident   meet

/iː/	/ə/	/e/
sleep	answer	help

WRITING

DISCUSSING THE BENEFITS OF DOING A PART-TIME JOB

1 Work in pairs. Match the pictures with the statements.

1 I love animals. ___ ☐
2 I spoke to people from different countries. ___ ☐
3 I had to work very quickly. ___ ☐
4 I learnt how to prepare different drinks. ___ ☐
5 I was very busy at lunchtime. ___ ☐

2 Read the question and underline the key words.

> Students can benefit from doing a part-time job. Discuss and give examples.

Now compare with your partner.

3 What should you include in your answer? Put the ideas in order of importance. 1 = not important to 5 = very important.

☐ earn money
☐ meet people
☐ become more confident
☐ develop your language skills
☐ get work experience

4 Read the student's answer and tick the things in activity 1 it mentions.

> There are many benefits of doing part-time work. First of all you can earn money. I worked in a cafe last year so I could buy extra books and clothes. Secondly, you can get useful work experience. My best friend worked as a zoo assistant at weekends. She loves animals so she decided to look for a job where she could work with them. Finally, you can develop your communication skills. We spoke to people from different countries so we had lots of opportunities to practise our English. I think that part-time work is a very good experience for students so I agree with the statement.

WRITING SKILLS

LINKING WITH SO

5 Look at the examples of *so* in the text. Read the sentence below and circle the correct answer.

We use *so* to a) give a reason / b) give a result.

6 Match the sentences. Then connect and rewrite them using *so*.

1 I fell very badly   **a** He passed all his exams.
2 He worked hard at school.   **b** I applied for the job.
3 I needed to earn some money.   **c** She left it.
4 She didn't like the job.   **d** I went to hospital.

7 Read the question and tick the things in activities 1 and 3 you can write about.

> Did you work during the holidays?
> What did you do? What did you learn from the experience! Tell us!

8 Write your answer to the question in activity 7.

GRAMMAR

1 Work in pairs. Student A, make questions using the words below. Student B turn to page 126 and answer Student A's questions.

1 What / name / of the building?
2 Where / be it?
3 Who / build it?
4 When / they / construct it?
5 What materials / they use / to construct it?
6 Why / be / it special?

2 Complete the sentences with *was, were, wasn't* and *weren't*.

The City Hall in Toronto, constructed in the 1960s, is one of the most famous buildings in Canada. However, the designer [1] _____ Canadian - he [2] _____ Finnish! His name [3] _____ Vijo Revell. The concrete and glass building [4] _____ popular at first. For many people, the two towers [5] _____ very strange but for other people the towers [6] _____ ugly –they were different and interesting! Today City Hall attracts many visitors!

3 Complete the sentences with the correct form of the words in brackets.

1 Vijo Revell _____ (design) the building.
2 Building workers and engineers _____ (use) concrete and glass to build it.
3 They _____ (construct) it in the nineteen sixties.
4 Many people _____ (not like) the building at first.
5 We really _____ (enjoy) our visit to City Hall. It was amazing!

VOCABULARY

1 Complete the sentences with these words.

concrete glass tall
fantastic unusual

4 Complete the sentences with the correct form of these words.

find tell learn meet spend

1 It was a very expensive holiday. We _____ a lot of money!
2 I _____ you about the trip. Don't you remember?
3 We _____ some really interesting people. We really enjoyed talking to them.
4 I _____ it difficult to get to City Hall. It was next to our hotel!
5 I really enjoyed my trip. It was really interesting and I _____ a lot about the city and the people.

5 Choose the correct phrases to complete the paragraph.

so visitors from all over the world come to see it
so they link the past and the present
so that future generations can enjoy them too
so old, stone or brick designs are special

Do you think it is important to protect and look after old buildings? Why?
I think that it is very important to protect old buildings in our towns and cities. Most of the buildings in my city are very modern [1] _____.
Old buildings are full of history [2] _____. The most spectacular building in my city is the cathedral. It is one of the largest cathedrals in the world [3] _____. It is a very important landmark and symbol of my city. In my opinion it is important to look after our old buildings [4] _____.

TORONTO

1 The Royal Bank Plaza is an amazing building with 14 000 mirrored _____ windows.

2 It is made of _____ and glass.

3 Trinity College is a _____ building, constructed in the 19th century.

4 CN Tower is a very _____ structure. It is 553 metres high!

5 The Sharp Centre for Design is interesting because it is different from any other building in the city – it is very _____.

2 Match the words with the definitions.

> wonderful   unusual   modern   huge   brick

1 something that is interesting because it is different: _____
2 the opposite of *old*: _____
3 something that is very large: _____
4 hard block of baked clay used to build houses: _____
5 something that is very good: _____

3 Complete the sentences with these verbs.

> apply for   earn   get   work   work as

1 Are you going to _____ a volunteer this year?
2 I want to enjoy my job and _____ some experience.
3 You can _____ good money here. It's a very good place to work.
4 We don't want to _____ full-time. We need time to study.
5 I think lots of people will _____ this job. It looks really interesting.

Bridge to IELTS

READING TEST PREPARATION

1 Work in pairs. Say what you know about the IELTS reading test.

2 Read the passage and tick the true sentences.

1 The test takes sixty minutes. ☐
2 The reading passages are short. ☐
3 It contains four reading texts. ☐
4 The reading passages are taken from advertisements. ☐
5 The test includes true/false/not given questions. ☐

Reading test

The first part of IELTS is the reading test. The test takes one hour and has three long reading passages. Students answer forty questions about the passages. The reading passages are from magazines, newspapers and academic articles.

There are many different questions including multiple choice; matching headings and paragraphs; completing a summary and true/false/not given questions. Students practise all of these types of question in *Bridge to IELTS*.

3 Work in pairs. Say how you prepare for the reading test outside class.

KEEPING VOCABULARY RECORDS

1 Work in pairs. Show each other how you remember new words.

2 Read the passage and complete the table.

All language students need a good vocabulary. There are many ways to learn and keep new words. Some students keep new words in a vocabulary notebook. Some like to keep them on cards. Other students keep them on their smartphone.

Some students like to write down the new words when they learn them (by date). Some like to put them in alphabetical order. Other students like to keep the new words by subject.

where to keep new words	how to organise them
notebook	³ _____: 10 September
¹ _____	alphabetically A, B, C
² _____	⁴ _____: festivals

3 Work in pairs. Say which things in the passage you would like to try.

4 For next lesson, write five new words and show your classmates how you keep them.

Unit 7
Urban sports

READING

1   Work in pairs. Ask and answer the questions.

   1   What games do you like to play?
   2   What sports do you like to do?
   3   What do you think an Urban Hunt is?

2   Read the passage and check your answer to activity 1 question 3.

3   Match the questions with the answers to the FAQs in the passage.

   a   Can I call friends for help?
   b   What happens in Urban Hunt?
   c   Do I have to solve the clues in order?
   d   How do I get around?
   e   Do we have to wear funny clothes?

4   Find words in the passage to complete the sentences.

   1   William went on an exciting _____, walking and camping in the mountains. (line 2)
   2   I'm not clever enough to do this crossword, it's a very difficult _____. (line 2)
   3   I can't find the answer to question 5 – can you give me a _____? (line 9)
   4   When you find a successful way to answer a problem, you _____ it. (line 25)

| Home | Event info | Directions | Contact |

URBAN HUNT

FAQs

Forty-seven teams came to Urban Hunt, Los Angeles for a day of fun, adventure and puzzles. In Urban Hunt, teams have to find answers to 12 questions before the other teams. The answers are all around
5 the city and you can phone your friends or use your smartphone to help you. The rules are simple – but completing Urban Hunt isn't!

1   _____
    You get a list of 12–15 clues. You have to
10 answer them and return to the starting point.

2   _____
    You can only travel on foot or by public transport. You can't use private transport.

3   _____
15 Sure. Teams often have friends near a PC ready to help. They can watch you on our interactive Urban Hunt map.

GRAMMAR

HAVE TO FOR OBLIGATION: CAN / CAN'T FOR PERMISSION

You use *have to* to say you are obliged to do something. You often use *have to* with rules.

*Teams **have to** find answers to 12 questions.*
*Do I **have to** solve the clues in order?*
Yes, you do. / No, you don't.

You use *don't have to* to say it's not necessary.

*You **don't have to** wear funny clothes.*

You use *can / can't* to talk about what you are allowed or not allowed to do.

*You **can** phone your friends or use your smartphone.*
*You **can't** use private transport.*
***Can** I call friends for help?*
*Yes, you **can**. / No, you **can't**.*

📖 **GRAMMAR REFERENCE PAGE 141**

4 Can I use my smartphone?
   Yes, you can but you don't need one to
20 answer the questions.

5 _____
   No, you don't have to wear funny clothes.
   Some teams do but it's not necessary.

6 _____
25 No, you don't. You can solve the clues in
   any order you like. You just have to find the
   quickest route around town.

1 **Read the passage again. Find five examples of *have to / don't have to* and seven examples of *can / can't*.**

2 **Choose the correct words.**

   1 Runners *have to / can't* drink a lot of water.
   2 Martina *can't / has to* come to the cinema on Friday, her mum won't let her.
   3 Our team *can / has to* go more quickly to win.
   4 Do we *have to / can* finish the hunt in one day?
   5 You *don't have to / can't* phone your friends. It's your choice.

3 **Complete the text with *can / can't* or the correct form of *(not) have to*.**

   Urban Hunt Rules

   In Urban Hunt you ¹ _____ solve all the clues before the other teams. You ² _____ use private transport like taxis or cars, but you ³ _____ use buses and trains or walk. You ⁴ _____ have a team member in their home to help you, but they ⁵ _____ leave their home. A lot of teams like to dress as movie characters, but teams ⁶ _____ do this.

4 **Write questions with *have to*.**

   1 you / do / homework this evening ?
   2 you / go to work on Monday ?
   3 you / meet anyone important tomorrow ?
   4 How often / you / come to class ?

PRONUNCIATION

STRONG AND WEAK FORMS: HAVE TO

1 🔊 1.39 **Listen to the answers to activity 4 and decide if the answers to 1–4 are strong /hævtuː/ or weak /hæftə/ forms of *have to*. Write S (strong) or W (weak).**

   1 ___   2 ___   3 ___   4 ___

   What is the rule? Choose the correct option.

   When another verb comes after, you /hævtuː/ / /hæftə/ (W) say it like this, but if there is no other verb, you don't /hævtuː/ / /hæftə/ (S).

2 **Work in pairs. Practise the questions in activity 4 and the answers.**

Discussion

Ask your partner four questions about what he / she has to do this evening / tomorrow / next week.

Listening

1 **■◀1.40 Listen to a team taking part in the Urban Hunt. Draw their route on the map.**

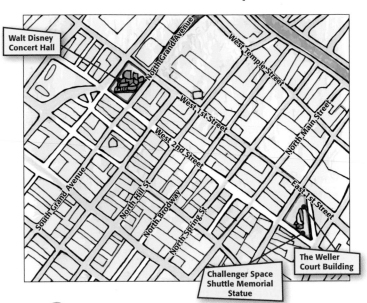

2 **■◀1.40 Listen again and choose the correct answers.**

1 What is the first clue about?
   a a statue of the space shuttle
   b a statue of an astronaut
   c a statue of a rocket

2 How can the team go to Little Tokyo?
   a by taxi   b by bus   c on foot

3 What do the team have to take?
   a a piece of the statue   b a photo   c a train

4 What do they think about the second clue?
   a It's easy.   b It's not easy or difficult.
   c It's difficult.

5 What is the answer to the next clue?
   a a cartoon   b a cinema   c a concert hall

6 Who has to go there?
   a Dee Dee   b the team
   c the Urban Hunt organisers

Discussion

Work in pairs. Discuss your answers to the questions.

1 Would you like to take part in Urban Hunt? Why / Why not?
2 What would you call your team?
3 What costumes would your team wear?

Vocabulary

Sports and sports skills

1 **Match the words below with the pictures.**

> balance   bounce   climb   hit   jump   kick

2 **Complete the phrases with the words in activity 1.**

1 _____ a building / a mountain
2 _____ over a wall
3 _____ a ball with your feet
4 _____ a ball with a racket
5 _____ on one leg
6 _____ the ball off a wall

3 **Put the sports into four groups.**

> judo   gymnastics   karate   climbing
> volleyball   basketball   golf   tennis

karate   *judo*   *gymnastics*   *climbing*

volleyball   *basketball*   *golf*   *tennis*

1 martial arts _____ _____
2 racket games _____
3 ball games _____ _____
4 other sports _____ _____

READING

1 Work in pairs. Look at the picture and say what you know about the sport of parkour.

2 Work in pairs. Guess the answers to the questions.

1 You do parkour …
   a in a sports hall. **b** on the street.
   c in the countryside.

2 It began in …
   a 2010. **b** 1990. **c** 1980.

3 It started in …
   a America. **b** France. **c** China.

4 The sport is like …
   a karate. **b** football. **c** climbing.

5 People do parkour …
   a in groups. **b** with a partner. **c** alone.

3 (3min) Read the passage in three minutes and check your answers to activity 2.

4 Read the passage again and match 1–5 with a–e.

1 Training with friends
2 Parkour is
3 Parkour is about
4 You can do parkour
5 Moves like jumping between roofs

a a sport you do in the city.
b is part of parkour.
c are difficult and look amazing.
d the way you move and think.
e in any clothes.

PARKOUR
– A NEW WAY OF THINKING ABOUT YOUR STREET

When you see a group of people running down a city street, jumping over everything in their path, you're looking at people doing parkour. Parkour is a mix of martial arts and gymnastics.

Parkour started in France in the 1980s. It is a way of getting from A to B. You do it by jumping over walls or climbing along buildings. But parkour isn't just about the physical moves. Parkour is a way of thinking about the world we live in and how we move around it. It is about freedom.

Where do people do parkour? It's easy! You can do parkour almost anywhere. What do you need to do the sport? Nothing! You don't need special equipment and you can do it in any clothes, although you need good training shoes when you're practising.

People do training for parkour in groups, and working on parkour moves with friends is an important part of the sport. People spend a lot of time doing exercises because they need to be fit and strong. They also need to have very good balance. But the sport isn't only about physical strength. Parkour needs very good concentration. You need to decide on your route quickly and you have to control your fear. Some parkour moves are very difficult, like jumping between roofs or bouncing from walls. And they look amazing. This is why many movies and games now show parkour and why many young people are trying the sport.

FOLLOWING THE SUBJECT OF A PASSSAGE

It's important to follow the subject of the passage. Read paragraph 3 again. See how many times *parkour* is referred to.

For example, you can do parkour almost anywhere.

You don't need special equipment to do the sport. You

can do it in any clothes, although you do need good

training shoes when you're practising (parkour).

GRAMMAR

NEED

You use *need* to say something is necessary.

*You **need** good training shoes.*
*You **don't need** special equipment.*

When you use *need* with another verb, you use the infinitive with *to*.

*You **need to decide** on your route quickly.*

📖 **GRAMMAR REFERENCE PAGE 141**

1 Look at the passage again and find five things you need to do and one thing you don't need to do.

2 Look at the table and write sentences for Urban Hunt with *need* and *don't need*.

✓		✗	
1	a good team leader	6	your car
2	a good map	7	to answer the questions in order
3	your mobile phone		
4	good walking shoes		
5	to be quick		

3 Work in pairs. Student A, turn to page 124. Student B, turn to page 126. Read the information. Then tell Student B about the sport or game.

Discussion

Work in pairs. Talk about a sport you enjoy. Say what it is and what you need to play it.

LISTENING

1 Look at the pictures and put the letters in order to make words.

1 gcclyin _____

2 wimsmign _____

3 kwanlig _____

4 joinggg _____

2 Work in pairs. Say …

- which activity / activities in activity 1 you do now.
- when you started.
- why you started.
- which activity you would like to try.

Bridge to IELTS

COMPLETING TABLES

In the listening test, you may be asked to complete
a table. Make sure you read the headings for the
rows and columns, as this helps you understand
the passage.

3 Label the picture with these words.

heart   lung   bone   muscle

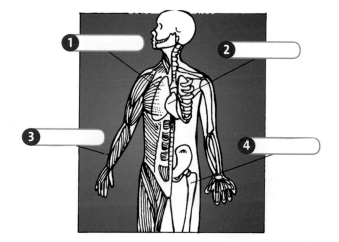

**4 🔊 1.41 Listen to a lecture about the activities in
activity 1. Tick the things each activity is good for.**

	heart	lungs	bones	muscles
walking	✓			
jogging				
swimming				
cycling				

**5 🔊 1.41 Listen again and complete the notes in the
table with one or two words or a number.**

walking	1	20% less than _____ years ago	2	Power walking is walking _____.
jogging	3	Improve your jogging time by _____ every week.	4	Find a jogging _____.
swimming	5	Swimming for _____ periods is very good.	6	Join a _____.
cycling	7	30 minutes of cycling uses _____ calories.	8	Good for people with a short distance to _____.

Discussion

**Work in pairs. Go round the class. Find out how
many students do the exercises in activity 1 and
how often.**

SPEAKING

MY FAVOURITE SPORT

1 Work in pairs. Look at the pictures and say where the sports are played. Use these words.

pitch   court   course

2 Work in pairs. Describe the sports in the pictures. Use the phrases below.

It's …	fun / exciting / fast / skilful
You need to …	concentrate / practise a lot / be fit / be quick / touch the ball
You have to …	
You can't …	

3 🔘 1.42 Listen to an interview. Which sport in activity 1 does the speaker talk about?

4 🔘 1.42 Listen again and choose the answers.

1 The game is played …
a on a court.   **b** in a pool.   **c** on a field.

2 The teams have … players.
a three   **b** six   **c** eleven

3 You hit the ball with your …
a head.   **b** feet.   **c** hands.

4 Valeria likes it because …
a it is difficult to play.
b you can play on the beach.
c it's fast and exciting.

Living IELTS

ADDING EMPHASIS (1)

🔘 1.43 Listen and underline the words that add emphasis to what the speaker is saying.

You can even play it on the beach.
You can play it in so many places.
I like such a lot of sports.
It's absolutely great!
It's very fast.
It's really easy to learn.

🔘 1.43 Listen and practise.

5 Think of your favourite sport. Make notes. Think about …

- what it is.
- where it is played.
- what the rules are.
- why you like it so much.

6 Work in pairs. Take turns to talk about the topic card. Use the notes you made in activity 5 to help you.

Describe your favourite sport.

You should talk about:
- what it is
- where it is played
- what the rules are
and explain why you like it so much.

WRITING

DESCRIBING A CHART

1 Work in pairs. Discuss the question. Use the ideas below.

Why do people do sports?	
to keep fit they are part of a club to meet other people to lose weight	for medical reasons to feel better it's fun

2 Look at the pie chart and read the paragraph describing it. Complete the chart with figures in the description.

Why people keep fit

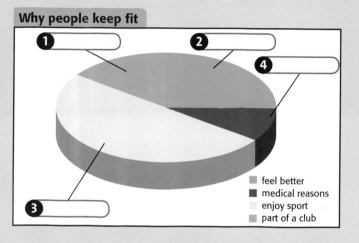

- ■ feel better
- ■ medical reasons
- □ enjoy sport
- ■ part of a club

The pie chart shows why people keep fit. The key at the side of the chart gives the reasons. Half of the people keep fit because they enjoy sports. Twenty-five per cent, or a quarter of people keep fit because it makes them feel better. One in ten people do exercise because of medical reasons. Finally, 15% of people keep fit because they are part of a club.

Bridge to IELTS

DESCRIBING FIGURES IN A CHART

When you write about a chart, you can use fractions or percentages to describe the figures.

50% = a half
33% = a third
25% = a quarter

WRITING SKILLS

LINKING WITH *BECAUSE*

3 Read the paragraph again and find four examples of *because*. Circle the correct words in the sentence below.

We use *because* to a) give a reason b) give a result.

4 Look at the pie chart and complete the sentences with the correct information using *because* + a reason.

Why young people don't do sport

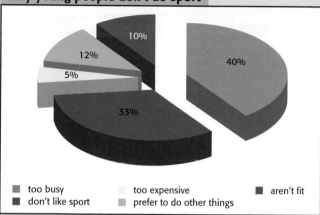

- ■ too busy
- ■ don't like sport
- □ too expensive
- ■ prefer to do other things
- ■ aren't fit

1 10% of young people don't do sport because …
2 5% don't do …
3 40% of young people …
4 A third of young people …
5 12% …

5 Look at the pie chart in activity 4. Make notes about it in the table.

the subject of the chart	what the chart shows	key information

6 Write a paragraph describing the chart in activity 4. Use the model in activity 2 and the notes you made in activity 5 to help you.

Unit 8
The natural world

VOCABULARY

LANDSCAPE FEATURES

1 **What can you see in the picture on the right? Label the pictures with the words below.**

> cliff   coast   rainforest   beach   river
> ocean   waves   waterfall

2 **Read the text and answer the questions.**

1 What is the name of the road?
2 Where is it?
3 Who built the road?
4 When did they complete it?
5 Why is it so special?

3 **Find words in the text for these definitions.**

1 s_____: the natural beauty that you see around you
2 d_____: the place where someone is going
3 l_____: everything you can see when you look across a large area of land
4 s_____: extremely beautiful to look at
5 u_____: different from anything else – the only one of its type

| HOME | PHOTO | VIDEOS | ABOUT US | CONTACT |

A

Introduction

Enjoy amazing scenery as you drive along the Great Ocean Road. For almost one hundred years, tourists have enjoyed this amazing road. It was built by soldiers between 1919 and 1932. The route along the south-eastern coast of Australia has become one of the world's most popular touring destinations. You have never seen landscapes like these! Enjoy spectacular views as the road goes along cliff tops, down to beaches, across rivers and waterfalls and through rainforests. It's a unique experience!

LISTENING

1 (2.1) **Listen to two friends, Leah and Erik, talking about the Great Ocean Road. Write L for Leah or E for Erik.**

1 ___ hasn't made holiday plans.
2 ___ has read a lot about the Great Ocean Road.
3 ___ has been to the south-east coast.
4 ___ has spent time in a rainforest.
5 ___ has never tried surfing.
6 ___ has always liked relaxing on the beach.

2 (2.1) **Listen again and choose T (true) or F (false).**

1 Erik went to the south-west coast last summer. T / F
2 He got lost when he was in the rainforest. T / F
3 He learned how to surf a few years ago. T / F
4 Leah last went to the zoo when she was a child. T / F

Living IELTS

COMMENTING

1 **Look at how to comment on what the other person said.**

Australia? Wow! That sounds great.
Surfing! That's exciting.

(2.2) **Listen and practise the phrases.**

2 **Work in pairs. Student A, choose an activity or a place and tell Student B you did it or went there. Student B, make a comment.**

Activity: surfing / bungee jumping / climbing
Place: New York / Singapore / Jeddah

VOCABULARY

ADJECTIVE AND NOUN COLLOCATIONS

1 **Look at the adjectives below. Match them with the words. There can be more than one answer.**

> thick   extinct   deep   spectacular
> sandy   snowy

1 _____ beach	4 _____ mountain
2 _____ river	5 _____ rainforest
3 _____ view	6 _____ volcano

2 **Complete the sentences. Use the adjective and noun collocations in activity 1.**

1 I've never been in such a _____!
   The trees are very close together so it's very dark!
2 You haven't learnt to swim so you need to keep away from the _____.
3 Look at the _____! Don't worry, it isn't active, so it isn't dangerous!
4 We stood on the cliff top and got a _____ of the landscape all around.
5 My idea of a perfect holiday is to lie on a _____ and enjoy the sound of the sea!
6 I love looking at the _____ in winter when the sun shines through the snow.

Discussion

Work in pairs. Discuss the questions.

1 Which of the places in Vocabulary activity 1 have you seen in your country?
2 Which place did you like most? Why?
3 Which places have you never seen?

GRAMMAR

PRESENT PERFECT SIMPLE + *EVER* AND *NEVER*; PAST SIMPLE

You use the present perfect simple to talk about past experiences when you don't say exactly when they happened. You often use the present perfect with *ever* and *never*.

I've been to Australia.
Have you ever been to the south-west coast?

You use the past simple to talk about the past when you give specific details, such as when, where, who with etc. You often use the past simple with a time expression.

Have you ever been to Australia? *Yes, I have.*
When did you go there? *I went* there *last year.*

 GRAMMAR REFERENCE PAGE 141

1 Choose the correct answers.

1 I *haven't been / didn't go* on holiday last year.
2 She lives near the Great Ocean Road so she *travelled / has travelled* on it many times.
3 You *haven't learnt / didn't learn* to drive so you can't drive my car!
4 We *haven't ever been / didn't ever go* to Australia but we'd like to go in future.
5 He *made / has made* a trip to the south coast a few years ago.

2 Complete the questions with *Have, Has* or *Did*.

1 _____ you ever travelled abroad?
2 _____ she like the landscapes she saw?
3 _____ many tourists been to your country?
4 _____ they take many photographs during their trip?
5 _____ he ever visited the rainforest?

3 Match the questions in activity 2 with the short answers.

a Yes, he has. He liked the different trees and plants there. _____
b No, I haven't. But I'm planning to go to Canada next summer. _____
c Yes, she did. She really liked the beautiful beaches. _____
d Yes, they did. They wanted to remember all the beautiful landscapes. _____
e Yes, they have. It's a very popular destination. _____

4 Complete the sentences with the past simple or present perfect form of the verbs in brackets.

1 What _____ you _____ (do) last weekend?
2 _____ you _____ (meet) your friends on Friday?
3 _____ you _____ (be) to any other countries?
4 When _____ you _____ (start) learning English?
5 _____ you _____ (watch) TV yesterday?
6 How many books _____ you _____ (read) in your life?

5 Answer the questions in activity 4 for you. Then work in pairs and compare your answers.

6 Put the words in order to make questions about an area of natural beauty.

1 called / it / What / is ?

_____

2 it / Where / is ?

_____

3 famous / Why / it / is ?

_____

4 changed / How / it / has ?

_____

7 Work in pairs. Student A, turn to page 125. Student B, turn to page 127. Read the information. Then ask and answer the questions in activity 6 about the places of natural beauty.

READING

1 Label the pictures with the words below.

kangaroo   platypus   dingo   fox   rabbit
water buffalo   cat

A ___   B ___   C ___   D ___

2 Work in pairs. Discuss the question.

Which of the animals and birds in activity 1 do you think are native to Australia?

Put the animals in two groups: a) *native to Australia* and b) *introduced to Australia*.

E ___   F ___   G ___

3 (3min) Read the passage in three minutes and check your guesses.

The changing environment of AUSTRALIA

A Australia is an amazing and beautiful country. But it also has something special which makes it very interesting for scientists. Australian plants and animals are very different from those of other continents. Because the continent was separate from the rest of the world for a very long time, many species evolved and developed that do not exist in other countries or which are uncommon. Examples include the kangaroo and the platypus. There are also 54 000 known species of insects, but scientists believe there are many others they haven't discovered.

B People have lived in Australia for a very long time. The native Aboriginal people respected the natural world. However, when Europeans came to Australia in the eighteenth century, their ways of life changed the country's landscapes and living things in harmful ways. Since the Europeans arrived, there has been a loss of 40% of total forest area and 75% of rainforests.

C These changes have resulted in the loss of many animal and plants. Eighteen species of mammal have already become extinct including the Tasmanian tiger and the desert rat kangaroo. At least thirty species have become endangered and at risk of extinction. The Europeans also brought many non-native animals, which have now run wild. These include foxes and cats which have become a danger to small native mammals and birds. Rabbits have destroyed massive areas of land and water buffalo have caused environmental damage in the rivers. The aboriginal people introduced the dingo, a kind of wild dog, but they have successfully adapted and become part of the native species.

4 Read the text again and circle TWO answers.

1 Which animals have developed over time in order to survive?
   a Tasmanian tigers   **b** kangaroos   **c** platypuses

2 When did Europeans come to Australia?
   a two hundred years ago   **b** in the eighteenth century
   c a few years ago

3 Which animals have attacked small mammals and birds?
   a foxes   **b** cats   **c** rabbits

4 Which animals did the Europeans introduce?
   a dingos   **b** cats   **c** rabbits

5 Match the phrases to make complete sentences.

1 Scientists   **a** have damaged agricultural land.
2 Water buffalos   **b** have died out.
3 Rabbits   **c** have caused harm to rivers.
5 Tasmanian tigers   **d** have discovered many insects.

6 Choose the correct answers.

1 If a plant or animal *evolves* (paragraph A) it …
   a develops slowly over a long period of time.
   b changes very quickly.

2 If you *respect* a place (paragraph B) you …
   a care about it.
   b don't have a high opinion of it.

3 If something is *harmful* (paragraph B) …
   a it is dangerous.
   b it is safe.

4 If an animal is *endangered* (paragraph C) …
   a it no longer exists.
   b it may not exist in future.

GRAMMAR

PRESENT PERFECT WITH *FOR* AND *SINCE*

You use the present perfect to talk about something which began in the past and continues up to now, with a present result.

*Eighteen species of mammal **have become** extinct.*

You use *for* when you give the period of time.

You use *since* when you give the beginning of the time.

*People have lived in Australia **for a very long time**.*
*Europeans have been in Australia **since the eighteenth century**.*

 GRAMMAR REFERENCE PAGE 141

1 Complete the sentences with *for*, *since* or *how long*.

 1 We use _____ to talk about the start of the action.
 2 We use _____ to talk about the time period of the action.
 3 We use _____ to ask about the period of time or start of the action.

2 Choose the correct answers.

 1 I haven't seen you for *a long time / January*.
 2 She's been in New Zealand since *two months / last year*.
 3 We haven't spent time at the beach for *weeks / the weekend*.
 4 He's lived in the area since *he was a child / many years*.
 5 They've known each other since *two weeks / Friday*.

3 Complete the sentences with *for* or *since*.

 1 We've been in Australia _____ a month.
 2 I've known them _____ I was a child.
 3 She's been interested in wildlife _____ many years.
 4 I haven't met many new people _____ I moved to the city.
 5 They've lived here _____ 2009.

PRONUNCIATION

STRONG AND WEAK FORMS: *HAVE* AND *HAS*

1 ⊙ 2.3 Listen to the sentences and mark the stressed (strong) sounds with a •.

 1 Have you ever been to Australia? ☐
 2 Yes, I have. ☐
 3 Has she ever seen a kangaroo? ☐
 4 No, she hasn't. ☐

2 Practise saying the sentences in the same way.

3 Student A, ask student B questions about things they have done, using the correct form of four of the verbs from the box. Student B, you don't have to give true answers!

> ride see eat drink make
> drive learn meet

A *Have you ever ridden an elephant?*
B *Yes, I have.*

Student A, say if you think the answer is true or not. Student B, now ask Student A questions, using the other four verbs.

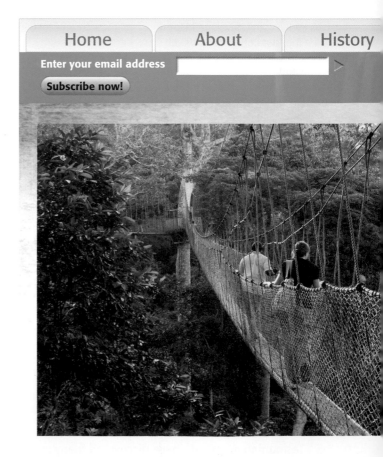

| Home | About | History |

Enter your email address ⬜ >
Subscribe now!

LISTENING

1 Work in pairs. Answer the questions.

1 What is a blog?
2 Have you ever written one?
3 Why do people enjoy reading blogs?

2 Read Caz's blog. Which picture best describes her trip?

3 Read the blog again and answer the questions.

1 Where has Caz been?
2 What did she do there?
3 Where is she now?
4 How does she feel about her experience?

4 🔊 2.4 Listen to Caz and her friend, Sergei, talking about the trip. Tick the things that Caz did.

went to the beach	☐
drove along the coast	☐
counted baby turtles	☐
went rafting	☐
read lots of books	☐
visited a volcano	☐
took lots of photographs	☐

5 🔊 2.4 Listen again and choose the correct answers.

1 How long did Caz spend in Costa Rica?
 a two weeks
 b two months
 c four weeks

2 How long has she been interested in animals?
 a since she was a child
 b for a few years
 c since last year

3 What did she enjoy doing most?
 a checking the nests
 b cleaning up the beach
 c counting the turtles

4 How did she feel about rafting?
 a it was dangerous
 b it was exciting
 c it was boring

5 Where did she spend her free time?
 a in the rainforest
 b relaxing on the beach
 c swimming in the sea

Discussion

Would you like to work on a conservation project like Caz? Why? / Why not?

Photos	Useful Links	Contact

Archives	2011	2010	2009	2008

October 30, 2011

Hi! I'm back in Sydney at last! My time on the sea turtle conservation project in Costa Rica in Central America was amazing! I've had the time of my life! I did a lot of work to protect turtles on the beach but I had some free time to explore the beautiful landscapes too!
I can't wait to tell you all about it!

Speaking

A special place of natural beauty

1 **Work in pairs. Ask and answer the questions.**

1 Does your country have a special area of natural beauty? If so, where is it?
2 What do people think of it?
3 Do you think it is important to protect areas of natural beauty? Why? / Why not?

2 🔘 **2.5** **Listen to Hiromi talking about Mount Fuji in Japan. Put the pictures in the order she talks about them.**

3 🔘 **2.5** **Listen again and choose the correct answers.**

1 Where is Mount Fuji?
 a in the north-west
 b in the south-east
 c in the south-west

2 How high is it?
 a less than 2 000 meters
 b less than 3 000 meters
 c more than 3 000 meters

3 When did she go there?
 a a few weeks ago
 b last July
 c when she was a child

4 What is special about it for her?
 a It changes colour.
 b It is peaceful to look at.
 c It is a symbol of peace.

4 **Think of a special place of natural beauty. Make notes about it. Think about …**

- what it is.
- where it is.
- what you know about it.
- why it is special for you.

Bridge to IELTS

Vocabulary range

Try to use as many adjectives as you can when you are describing a place. This will show the examiner that you have a good range of vocabulary.

5 **Work in pairs. Take turns to talk about the topic card.**

Describe a special place of natural beauty.

You should say:
- what it is
- where it is
- if you have been there
and explain why it is special for you.

WRITING

THE ADVANTAGES AND DISADVANTAGES OF TOURISM

1 Work in pairs. Look at the pictures of a beach resort. What advantages and disadvantages do you think tourism has brought to the local area? Use the words below.

animals and plants	jobs
buildings	money
crowded	pollution
damage to the environment	

2 Read the paragraph and choose the best title.

a What tourists can learn from other countries
b Why people go on holiday
c The advantages and disadvantages that tourists bring

Many tourists want to visit areas of natural beauty. They want to enjoy beautiful landscapes, such as sandy beaches and palm trees. There are one or two advantages to tourism.
A _____), local people can earn money on the beach selling souvenirs. Tourists like spending money when they are on holiday!
B _____), tourists can bring disadvantages too. **C** _____), new hotels and buildings can damage the natural environment. Also planes and buses are noisy.
D _____), tourists bring more disadvantages than advantages.

WRITING SKILLS

PRESENTING AN ARGUMENT

3 Look at the text again and put these words in the correct place, A–D.

In my opinion   However   For example   First of all

4 Complete the sentences with the correct words and phrases from activity 3.

1 There are some benefits to staying in a hotel. _____, it is very comfortable and secondly it is very convenient.

2 There are many places of natural beauty to visit in Britain, _____ the Lake District and the Forest of Dean.

3 Some people think that we have too many holidays. _____ they are good because it is important for people to have time to relax.

4 Tourism can bring jobs and money to an area. _____ we need to do more to protect areas of natural beauty.

5 Group these ideas under two headings: advantages and disadvantages.

1 jobs for local people – hotels, restaurants and shops

2 more people – crowded – more buses and cars

3 sand dunes cleared – new hotels and buildings

4 tourists bring money into an area

6 Match the sentences a–d with the ideas in activity 5.

a This can cause pollution.
b This can destroy the habitat of animals and plants.
c This can improve local services, like schools and hospitals.
d They have more money for their families.

7 Read the essay title and write a paragraph about it. Use the model in activity 2 and the ideas in activities 5 and 6 to help you. Use *First of all, For example, However* and *In my opinion*.

Tourists cause more harm than good to local people and the environment. Do you agree or disagree?

Family

READING

1 Work in pairs. Describe what you can see in the pictures on this page. Use the words below.

> eggs   envelope   ginger   guests   parent   baby

2 Read the passage and choose the correct answers.

1 The party is celebrated in …
   a Japan.
   b Britain.
   c China.

2 It is celebrated when a baby …
   a is one month old.
   b is one year old.
   c starts to walk.

3 Babies are given …
   a red envelopes.
   b ginger.
   c red eggs.

4 The colour red is associated with …
   a happiness.
   b health.
   c success.

A baby's first month birthday is a special event in China and is celebrated with a special party. It is called a Red Egg and Ginger party and friends and relatives are invited. The
5 guests bring presents for the baby. These presents include red envelopes containing 'lucky money'. The guests are given presents by the baby's parents too. These are usually red coloured eggs with a little bit of ginger.
10 The eggs are coloured red because the colour red means happiness in China. Ginger also has a meaning — it
15 represents a balance between cold and warm!

3 Find words in the passage with the following meanings.

1 r_____ : members of your family (line 4)
2 g_____ : a person who is invited to a special event (line 5)
3 l_____ : something that brings good luck (line 7)
4 m_____ : the thing or idea that something represents (line 14)

GRAMMAR

PRESENT SIMPLE PASSIVE

You use the passive form when you are interested in the action, not the person or people who did it. You form the present simple passive with the present of the verb *be* and the past participle.

It is called a Red Egg and Ginger party.
Friends and relatives are invited.

You can use *by* to say who or what does something.

The guests are given presents by the baby's parents.

 GRAMMAR REFERENCE PAGE 142

1 Write the past participle forms of the verbs below.

> celebrate   call   colour   give
> invite   make   hold   wear

2 Complete the sentences with *is, isn't, are* or *aren't*.

1 Red Egg and Ginger parties _____ celebrated in China.
2 The party _____ held when a baby is one year old.
3 Babies _____ given blue envelopes.
4 A present _____ given to each guest.
5 The eggs _____ coloured red.

3 Put the words in order to make sentences.

1 by / presents / The baby's parents / given / the guests / are .
2 lucky envelopes / given / Babies / are / the guests / by .
3 the parents / Each guest / given / is / a red egg / by .
4 Each egg / by / coloured red / is / the parents .

4 Complete the text with the present simple passive form of the verbs in brackets.

A girl's fifteenth birthday is a special event in Latin America and ¹ _____ (celebrate) with a special party. It ² _____ (call) *Quinceañera*, and friends and relatives ³ _____ (invite). The girl wears a pink or white dress. The girl's father ⁴ _____ (give) flowers, usually roses. Fifteen candles ⁵ _____ (give) by the girl to fifteen guests. The candles represent people who have been important to the girl in her life so far.

LISTENING

1 ◯2.6 Listen to two friends, Jing and Fouad, talking about a Red Egg and Ginger party. Choose the correct answers.

1 Red Egg and Ginger Parties are often held …
   a in a restaurant.
   b at home.

2 Eggs represent …
   a family.
   b change.

3 It is believed that tigers …
   a look after babies.
   b teach parents how to care for their babies.

4 Presents are usually given …
   a at the start of the party.
   b at the end of the party.

2 ◯2.6 Listen again. Match the beginnings and endings to make sentences about Jing's family.

1 Her grandmother	a is an engineer.
2 Her nephew	b is twenty-six years old.
3 Her brother	c is very funny.
4 Her sister-in-law	d looks very happy.
5 Her parents	e live in Beijing.

3 Underline the correct information.

1 Jing's parents have *two / three* children.
2 Her brother *has / hasn't* done military service.
3 Her brother met his wife *many years ago / one year ago*.
4 Her mother learnt to drive at the age of 52 / 62!
5 Her nephew is *one month / one year* old.

Discussion

Work in pairs. Discuss the questions.

1 In which order do you do these things in your country?
   • have children
   • learn to drive
   • get married
   • do military service
   • leave school

2 Which of these things have you done? Which would you like to do in the future?

VOCABULARY

FAMILY RELATIONSHIPS

1 Look at the family relationship words below and put them in three groups: *male, female* and *both*.

> father   aunt   grandmother
> nephew   cousin   parents
> children   brother-in-law
> mother   son   niece   daughter
> sister-in-law   uncle   grandfather

2 Find pairs of words. Which word has no pair?

3 Complete the sentences with words from activity 1.

1 Your mother and father are your _____.
2 Your brother's son is your _____.
3 Your father's sister is your _____.
4 Your father's mother is your _____.
5 Your sons and daughters are your _____.
6 Your sister's husband is your _____.

4 Choose the correct answers.

1 I really like my parents' parents – especially my *grandfather / uncle*.
2 My mother has two brothers so I've got two *uncles / nephews*.
3 Both my aunt and uncle have children so I've got lots of *cousins / sisters*.
4 I don't see my *nephew / niece* very often because my sister and her daughter live in Canada.

5 Choose the odd one out.

1 grandfather	son	cousin	nephew
2 parents	daughter	children	grandparents
3 aunt	niece	brother	mother
4 son	cousins	parents	children

6 Work in pairs. Choose three members of your family and tell each other about them.

READING

1 Work in pairs. Look at the pictures above and on page 79 and discuss the questions.

1 Where do you think the people live?
2 How old do you think the people are?
3 Which of these things can help you live a long life?
- [ ] diet
- [ ] exercise
- [ ] positive attitude
- [ ] clean environment
- [ ] relationships
- [ ] sleep

2 Guess the answers, a, b or c.

1 The place in the picture is in …
   a Brazil.
   b Japan.
   c Pakistan.

2 A 'Blue Zone' is …
   a surrounded by water.
   b where people live for a long time.
   c in the countryside.

3 The place in the picture is …
   a easy to get around.
   b a good place to grow things.
   c famous for animals.

3 Read Paragraph A of the passage on page 79 and check your guesses.

4 Read the whole passage and tick the ideas in activity 1 that are mentioned.

Living in the Blue Zone

A A 'Blue Zone' is a name for a place where people live longer, healthier lives. The Hunza Valley is in the North of Pakistan. It is a place where people can live until the age of 90 in good health. Some people even get to the age of 120! The Hunza Valley is a rich, fertile area with a lot of farms. The region is located high up in the mountains and is isolated from the rest of the world.

B No one really knows how long the people of the Hunza valley live. The truly extraordinary fact is that all studies of the Hunza show that the older people are fit, healthy and full of energy. The mountain areas where they live are extremely rough and their lives are spent moving between the steep mountains and rocky valleys. The people here are fitter and healthier than even the famous Sherpa people of the Himalaya region.

C The Hunza people have a simple lifestyle and eat mostly plants, which are eaten raw. They don't have large amounts of fuel for cooking food and there aren't many animals available for eating so they plant what they can and gather the rest. Apricots, cherries and other fruits are all grown by the Hunza. They also eat a lot of grains including wheat and barley.

D The Hunza people are described by some researchers as 'the happiest people on earth'. This is because they have a positive outlook. Perhaps their love of life can be explained by their daily exercise and simple way of living.

5 **Read the text again and match ideas 1–4 with paragraphs A–D.**

1	what is known about their diet	A
2	what can be learned from the Hunza people	B
3	where the Hunza valley is situated	C
4	how they remain in good health	D

6 **Choose T (true) or F (false).**

1 Most of the Hunza people survive to the age of 120.   T / F
2 The Hunza people are less healthy than the Sherpa people.   T / F
3 The Hunza people mostly eat fruit and vegetables.   T / F
4 The Hunza people have a positive view of life.   T / F

7 **Choose the correct meaning for the words in the text.**

1 If land is *fertile* (paragraph A) …
   a plants grow well there.
   b plants cannot survive there.

2 If a place is *isolated* (paragraph A) …
   a it is far from other areas.
   b it is near other places.

3 If something is *extraordinary* (paragraph B) it is …
   a very unusual.
   b not very interesting.

4 If something is *raw* (paragraph C) …
   a it tastes good.
   b it is not cooked.

5 If you have a *positive outlook* (paragraph D) …
   a you feel happy about life.
   b you feel life is very difficult.

GRAMMAR

PASSIVE AND ACTIVE VERBS

1 Look at these two sentences from the passage on page 79. What's the difference between them?

1 *The Hunza people have a simple lifestyle.*
2 *Plants are eaten raw.*

In which sentence are we more interested in the people?

In which sentence is the action more important than the people?

📖 **GRAMMAR REFERENCE PAGE 142**

2 Rewrite the sentences using the present simple passive form. Use *by* if necessary.

1 They grow fruit in the valley.
Fruit _____.

2 They spend their lives moving around.
Their lives _____.

3 Doctors examine them in the hospital.
They _____.

4 They eat a lot of fruit and vegetables.
A lot _____.

3 Complete the text with the passive or active form of the verbs in brackets.

Vilcabamba is a small village in Southern Ecuador. It ¹ _____ (locate) in a high valley. People who live there ² _____ (know) for having a very healthy lifestyle. Vegetables ³ _____ (pick) fresh from the garden and ⁴ _____ (eat) on the same day. Becoming old ⁵ _____ (see) in a positive way and people ⁶ _____ (give) more respect as they grow older.

Discussion

Work in pairs. Discuss the questions.

1 Would you like to live in a Blue Zone like the Hunza valley? Why? / Why not?

2 Do you agree that the Hunza are 'the happiest people on earth'? Why? / Why not?

LISTENING

1 Look at the picture. Label the items with the words below.

kimono   sleeve   belt   sandals   scarf

2 Complete the sentences with the words in activity 1.

1 A _____ is a thin piece of material worn around your waist.

2 _____ are light open shoes which are worn when the weather is warm.

3 A _____ is a traditional, formal dress worn by women in Japan.

4 A _____ is one of the two parts of an item of clothing that covers the arm.

5 A _____ is a long piece of cloth that is worn around the neck.

3 🔘 2.7 Listen to Hiromi describing a special event in her country. Choose T (true) or F (false).

1 The ceremony is for young people who are 20 years old.   T / F

2 Kimonos are usually worn by young women.   T / F

3 Kimonos worn by young women have short sleeves.   T / F

4 The belt is not very beautiful.   T / F

5 The most expensive item of the dress is the belt.   T / F

4 🔘 2.7 Listen again and choose the correct answers.

1 When is the ceremony held?
a on 1 January
b on 2 of January
c in the second week in January

2 What kind of kimono is worn by older women?
a with short sleeves
b with no sleeves
c with long sleeves

3 Who are speeches given by?
a parents
b government officials
c teachers

4 What are young people given during the ceremony?
a sweets
b jewellery
c money

5 After the ceremony, where are celebrations held?
a at home with family
b in bars with friends
c at college with friends and family

5 Complete the text. Write no more than one word in each gap.

The coming of age ceremony is celebrated by all young people of the age of ¹ _____ and takes place on the second ² _____ in January. Girls wear a special kimono with a ³ _____, which is called an *obi*. After the ceremony, they go to bars or ⁴ _____ and celebrate with friends.

6 Put the words in order to make questions about a coming of age ceremony.

1 celebrated / it / is / Where ?
2 it / celebrates / Who ?
3 it / At what age / is / celebrated ?
4 happens / at the ceremony / What ?

7 Work in pairs. Student A, turn to page 125. Student B, turn to page 127. Read the information. Then ask and answer the questions you wrote in exercise 6.

Speaking

An important life event

1 **Work in pairs. Ask and answer the questions.**

   1 When do you become an adult in your country?
   2 At what age can you do the things in the pictures?

2 🔊 2.8 **Listen to Ana talking about an important life event. Which picture is she talking about?**

3 🔊 2.8 **Listen again and choose the correct answers.**

   1 In Brazil you can start driving at the age of …
   a 16.　　　**b** 17.　　**c** 18.

   2 A driving licence is given to people who pass …
   a one test.　　**b** two tests.　**c** a number of tests.

   3 A driving licence is considered to be a sign of …
   a independence.　**b** success.　**c** intelligence.

Living IELTS

Adding emphasis (2)

1 🔊 2.9 **Listen and underline the words that add emphasis to what the speaker is saying.**

I do think that getting a driving licence is a very important life event in Brazil.
It's far from easy.
It really does take a very long time.
I really do think that it can be compared to a very long journey.
What I like most is the independence it brings.
It's a truly fantastic feeling!

🔊 2.9 **Listen again and practise.**

2 **Complete the sentences with the words and phrases.**

   do　does　far　truly　what I like most is　really

   1 _____ is used for emphasis with the word *from* + adjective.
   2 Auxiliary verbs like _____ and _____ are used in the positive to add emphasis.
   3 Adding the word _____ before the auxiliary also adds emphasis.
   4 If we want to emphasise that we like something more than anything else we can use a sentence that begins with a _____ clause.
   5 Words like 'really' and _____ can add emphasis to adjectives.

4 **Think of an important life event. Make notes about it. Think about …**

   - what it is.
   - when it happens.
   - how you prepare for it.
   - why it is so important.

Bridge to IELTS

Structuring your talk

The phrases on the task card are called *prompts*. You can use the prompts to structure your answer. Try to turn the phrases into questions to help you answer. Remember that the examiner will ask you one or two *rounding off* questions after you finish.

5 **Work in pairs. Take turns to talk about the topic card. Use the notes you made in activity 4 to help you.**

Describe an important life event in your country.

You should say:
- what it is
- when it happens
- how you prepare for it
and explain why it is so important.

WRITING

DESCRIBING A TABLE

1 Match the pictures with the words below. Which part of the wedding is more expensive in your country?

1 wedding ceremony
2 honeymoon
3 wedding reception

2 Look at the table and underline the best title.

A The honeymoon is not expensive
B The costs of an average wedding in the UK
C The costs of a wedding reception

wedding cake	£370
wedding dress	£1 790
presents	£205
photographer	£1 810
ceremony	£520
reception	£5 690
flowers	£685
entertainment	£850
wedding rings	£630
honeymoon	£3 100

WRITING SKILLS

COMPARING FIGURES IN A TABLE

3 Read the description of the table in activity 2 and choose the correct words.

The table shows the amount of money spent on a typical wedding in the UK. The most money is spent on the ¹ reception / ceremony. It costs almost six ² hundred / thousand pounds.

This is twice the cost of the ³ honeymoon / wedding cake. The wedding rings and the ⁴ flowers / honeymoon cost almost the same. Couples spend more on entertainment than they do on the ⁵ wedding dress / wedding cake. ⁶ Flowers / Presents are the least expensive items.

4 Look again at the table in activity 2. Complete the sentences with the words below.

almost the same   costs almost   more
the most   twice the cost   the least

1 The reception is _____ expensive item.
2 The entertainment _____ £900.
3 Couples spend _____ money on presents.
4 The wedding dress and the photographer cost _____.
5 The wedding dress is _____ of the entertainment.
6 Couples spend _____ on wedding rings than they do on the ceremony.

5 Look at the table. Write sentences about the items.

1 the reception / the most
2 the reception / twice the cost / the honeymoon
3 the wedding cake / almost the same / the presents
4 the reception / almost / $10 000
5 the flowers / more / the wedding dress
6 presents / the least

The costs of an average wedding in Canada	
wedding cake	$524
wedding dress	$1 798
presents	$457
photographer	$2 414
reception	$9 572
flowers	$1 334
entertainment	$1 264
wedding rings	$2 718
honeymoon	$5 287

6 Write a paragraph describing the table in activity 5. Use the model in activity 3 and the sentences you wrote in activity 5 to help you.

GRAMMAR

1 Complete the text with the correct form of the verbs in brackets.

A baby's first birthday is an important event in Malta. It ¹ _____ (celebrate) with a special party. It ² _____ (call) *Il-quccija* and friends and family ³ _____ (invite). Several objects ⁴ _____ (place) on the floor in front of the baby. Each object has a meaning and they ⁵ _____ (include) a pen for a writer, a thermometer for a doctor and money for a business person. Other objects ⁶ _____ (add) too. The object the baby ⁷ _____ (touch) first will become important in his or her life in future.

2 Complete the paragraph with these phrases.

> In my opinion   However   for example
> First of all   because

Many people choose to go to a gym to take exercise ¹ _____ they want to keep fit and healthy. ² _____ many gyms have good facilities and equipment, ³ _____ , running machines and weights. They are also very good places to meet people and have fun. ⁴ _____ gyms have some disadvantages too. Some of them are very expensive and sometimes they are located too far away. ⁵ _____ , gyms are good places to exercise.

VOCABULARY

1 Complete the words.

1 Viktor is my sister's son. He's my n _ _ _ _ w.
2 Ziyoda is my brother's wife. She's my s _ _ _ _ _ _ - _ _ - _ _ w.
3 Emilio is my father's son. He's my b _ _ _ _ _ r.
4 Bogdan is the son of my father's brother. He's my c _ _ _ _ n.
5 Jing is my sister's daughter. She's my n _ _ _ e.
6 Ana is my father's sister. She's my a _ _ t.

2 Put the words below in the correct place in the scale.

> mother   grandson   grandparent   daughter

older ←——————————————————→ younger

3 Match the verbs with the nouns to make collocations.

1	have	**a** school
2	learn	**b** married
3	get	**c** to drive
4	do	**d** military service
5	leave	**e** children

4 Choose the correct answers.

1 It was a *spectacular / thick* forest. It was so difficult to see through the trees we nearly got lost!
2 The volcano is very safe to climb – it's *deep / extinct*.
3 The water is very *deep / snowy* so be very careful.
4 We had a *spectacular / sandy* view of the coastline from the top of the cliff.
5 Our hotel was near a *deep / sandy* beach so we spent most of our time lying in the sun.

WRITING TEST PREPARATION

1 Work in pairs. Write three things you know about the IELTS writing test.

2 Read the passage and check your answers.

Writing test

The writing test is the third part of IELTS. There are two parts to the writing test, task 1 and task 2. You have one hour to complete the writing test. In task 1, students write 150 words about information in a graph, a table or a diagram. In task 2, students write 250 words about an essay title. The essay title often asks students to discuss a topic. In general, you should take 20 minutes for task 1 and forty minutes for task 2. Students practise answering these types of tasks in *Bridge to IELTS*.

3 Work in pairs. Say how you can prepare for the writing test outside class.

Study Skills

USING REFERENCE MATERIALS

1 Answer the quiz.

What does a good dictionary include?

a	how to pronounce the word	☐
b	American or British English	☐
c	what kind of word it is (verb, noun, adjective)	☐
d	where the word comes from	☐
e	if the word is regular or irregular	☐
f	different meanings of the word	☐
g	anything different about the word	☐
h	words with similar meanings	☐

2 Check your answers in the passage.

What do you do when you need to find the meaning of a new word? Ask your teacher? Ask another student? Do you look at your smartphone or electronic dictionary? Do you look at an online dictionary or do you use a paper dictionary?

A good dictionary has a lot of information. Of course it tells you the meaning of the word. It also tells you how to pronounce the word and if the word is British or American. It gives you grammar information like what kind of word it is. Is the word irregular or regular, is there is anything different about the word, for example, is it uncountable or countable?

Unfortunately, it doesn't tell you where the word comes from or other words with similar meanings.

3 Work in pairs. Check your dictionaries to see if they have the things in activity 1.

Unit 10
Conservation

READING

1 Work in pairs. Look at the picture below and say what you think Earth Day is about. Use these phrases …

- protecting the environment
- saving energy
- controlling pollution
- cleaning up waste
- recycling
- helping animals

2 Read the webpage and decide which of these things it is for.

a to tell a story
b to ask people to do things
c to give a warning

TAKE ACTION | DONATE | NEWSROOM | PROGRAMS | ABOUT US

Do something for Earth Day

Help us celebrate Earth Day by organising an Earth Day event. There are many things you can do to have fun and change things on your campus. Here are some ideas …

- plant trees
- have a recycling competition
- clean up litter with students and staff
- organise an Earth Day party
- hold an Earth Day concert with the other students.

3 Read the webpage again and choose T (true) or F (false).

On Earth Day students can …
1 change things around the university.   T / F
2 remove rubbish.   T / F
3 have a concert with the staff.   T / F

4 Find words in the text which mean …
1 something important, interesting, or unusual that happens: _____
2 to put a tree in the ground to grow: _____
3 to mark a special day: _____
4 when a person or a group tries to be better than the others to win a prize: _____

LISTENING

1 ⊙2.10 **Listen to three students planning an Earth Day event. Match their names with the ideas they suggest.**

Alex   organize a clean-up
Esra   give out leaflets
Carol   plant trees

2 ⊙2.10 **Listen again and complete the sentences with no more than two words or a number.**

The Ecology Society didn't celebrate Earth Day last [1] _____; Earth Day is [2] _____ months away from the meeting. They think a concert is a good idea but difficult [3] _____.
They decide to have a campus [4] _____ and collect litter.

GRAMMAR

COUNTABLE AND UNCOUNTABLE NOUNS / *SOME* AND *ANY*

Countable nouns have a singular and plural form.

tree – trees, month – months, band – bands
*There is **a tree**. There are **two trees**.*

Uncountable nouns only have a singular form.

*There **is some** money.*

You use *some* with statements.

*We put up **some** posters.*

You use *any* with questions and negatives.

*We don't have **any** posters.*
*Is there **any** money?*

📕 *GRAMMAR REFERENCE PAGE 142*

1 Put the words below into two groups: countable and uncountable.

> music   problem   idea   month
> time   student   litter   person

2 Choose the correct words.
1 I've got *some / any / a* posters here for the Campus Clean-up.
2 Are there *some / any / a* volunteers?
3 There are *some / any / a* people waiting at the main building.
4 Did you bring *some / any / a* bag to put litter in?
5 No, I didn't know you wanted me to bring *some / any / a* bags.

3 Complete the sentences with *some* or *any*.
1 Alex, do you have _____ ideas for the Earth Day party?
2 I've spent _____ time thinking about it.
3 _____ people are here to help organise the party.
4 Have we got _____ money? I'd like to buy some coffee for them.

4 Work in pairs. Student A, turn to page 125. Student B, turn to page 127. Write questions and answers. Then ask and answer questions about the Earth Day party.

READING

1 **Work in pairs and discuss the questions.**

1 How many times have you used water today?
2 What did you use it for?

2 **Read the information about river life. Label the picture with the highlighted words.**

River life

From the mighty Amazon in the **jungles** of South America to the Danube in the **hills** and **forests** of central Europe, rivers cross our earth. A **river** often starts near **mountains** at a **lake** or **stream** and all rivers run into the sea. Rivers are important sources of food and water and this is why many great cities are built near rivers.

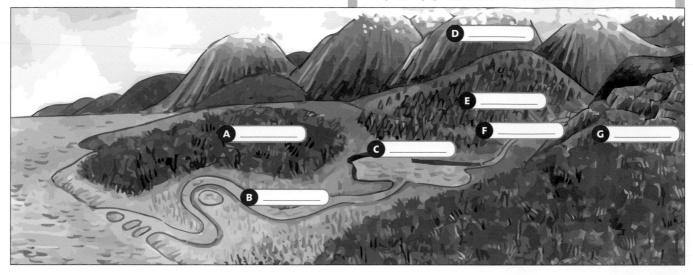

3 **Look at the title of the passage. Which of these things do you think will be mentioned in the text?**

a pollution in rivers
b how to find fresh water
c water in the desert
d dirty water and illness

4 **Read the passage and check your ideas in activity 3.**

Bridge to IELTS

USING INFORMATION FOR PREDICTING

Thinking about the ideas in the passage before you read can help you to understand it. Look at the title, any pictures, numbers or headings to help you before you read it the first time.

A difficult balance – how we are managing fresh water supplies

Rivers are beautiful and important parts of the landscape. Over five billion people need them, as well as thousands of animals. But water supplies in countries all over the world are decreasing and river
5 pollution is increasing.

Today, even the world's great rivers like the Nile, Yangtze and Ganges are in danger, with 30 out of 47 of the largest rivers showing water pollution. Some of the most polluted rivers are in Europe and the United
10 States. There isn't much clean water left and the cleanest rivers are a long way from humans, in the Arctic or Siberia.

The situation in the Middle East is a good example of how we are using water too much. In the 1970s,
15 Saudi Arabia wanted to produce food for its people. To do this, they needed water. But how much water does the country have? In a year it only has 100 mm of rain. To get water, engineers drilled down into the rock. How many years did they have before the
20 water ran out? It took just 20 years to use all the underground water.

5 **Read the passage again and choose the correct answers.**

1 What is the writer's attitude?
   a positive
   b not positive and not negative
   c negative

2 Where are the clean rivers?
   a in Europe
   b in America
   c a long way from people

3 How did people get water in the desert?
   a from rain
   b by drilling
   c by buying it from other countries

4 What is the problem?
   a There is too much water.
   b There are too many people and not enough water.
   c There isn't enough food.

25 All over the world, people are suffering because of the problems caused by growing populations and falling water supply. For the first time in history, food production from agriculture is dropping, and nothing can help to stop this. Each day brings 10 000 more people to feed with less water to do this. We haven't got much time. We have to clean up our rivers – and fast.

6 **Find these words in the passage and match them with their definitions.**

> pollution (line 5)   drill (line 18)
> cause (line 23)   agriculture (line 25)

1 farming and growing food: _____
2 something that makes things dirty: _____
3 to make a hole in something: _____
4 to make something happen: _____

GRAMMAR

HOW MUCH / HOW MANY

You use *how much* with uncountable nouns and *how many* with countable nouns.

How much water *does the country have?*
How many years *did they have before the water ran out?*

 GRAMMAR REFERENCE PAGE 142

1 **Choose the correct words.**

1 How *much / many* rivers are polluted?
2 How *much / many* rain falls in Saudi Arabia in a year?
3 How *much / many* years did the underground water in Saudi Arabia last?
4 How *much / many* people are born every day?

2 **Find the answers to the questions in activity 1 in the reading passage.**

3 **Complete the sentences with *how much* or *how many*.**

1 _____ clean water is on earth?
2 _____ people live in your city?
3 Can you remember _____ time it took to read the passage?
4 _____ money do you spend every day?

4 **Work in pairs. Student A, turn to page 125. Student B, turn to page 127. Write the questions. Then ask and answer the questions.**

Discussion

Say which information in activity 4 surprised you or interested you.

Listening

1   **Work in pairs. Look at the photos and say what you know about the animals. Think about …**

- where they live
- what they eat
- do they live in groups or alone
- which are in danger.

2 **Complete the sentences with the words in the box.**

> habitat   extinct   resource   destruction

1 When all the animals of one group are dead, they are _____.
2 An animal's _____ is the place it naturally lives in.
3 Something like oil, that we use to make other things, is a valuable _____.
4 The _____ of something is when it is damaged so badly it cannot be used.

3 **Match these possible causes of danger with the animals in activity 1.**

> hunting   river pollution   climate change destroying habitat   oil pollution

4 🔘 2.11 **Listen to a Professor talking about the Red List. Check your answers to activity 3.**

5 🔘 2.11 **Listen again and choose the correct answers.**

1 The Red List is a list of …
   a animals in danger.
   b polluting countries.
   c things to remember.
2 Mountain gorillas live in …
   a Brazil.
   b China.
   c Africa.
3 There are around … mountain gorillas today.
   a 1 800
   b 800
   c 8 000
4 Black rhino numbers decreased by …
   a 9%.
   b 19%.
   c 96%.
5 Polar bears are dying because they …
   a don't have enough time to find food.
   b are too warm.
   c are too slow to hunt.

6 **Choose T (true) or F (false).**

1 Human activity is making more animals extinct. T / F
2 Chemicals are causing illness in dolphins.   T / F
3 Mountain gorillas are in danger from pollution. T / F
4 Products made from black rhino are very popular.   T / F

Bridge to IELTS

UNDERSTANDING LONG LISTENING PASSAGES

When you are listening to a long listening passage, listen for words and phrases like these that tell you how many ideas or parts are in it.
The first part of my talk is about …
The next thing to talk about is …
Let's look at three threats …
First / Second / Third

VOCABULARY

WORD FORMATION

1 **You can sometimes tell whether a word is a noun, verb or adjective from its ending.**

destroy ➜ *destruction (noun)*

2 **Make nouns from these words.**

1 pollute _____
2 conserve _____
3 extinct _____

PRONUNCIATION

WORD STRESS IN VERBS AND NOUNS

1 🔘 2.12 **Listen and check your answers to activity 2. Is the stress on each word:**

   a on the first syllable?
   b on the last syllable?
   c on the syllable before *-tion*?

2 🔘 2.12 **Listen again and practise saying the words.**

Discussion

Work in groups. Choose three ways to help animals on the Red List:

• put them into zoos
• make hunting against the law
• create nature parks
• make destroying the animals' habitat illegal
• reduce global warming.

SPEAKING

AN ENVIRONMENTAL PROBLEM

1 Look at the pictures. Say what they show. Use the words below.

> pollution   destruction   climate change
> global warming   recycling

2 Work in pairs. Decide which of these things are the three most important causes of global warming. Then turn to page 125 and check your ideas.

> industry   power stations   transport   agriculture
> cutting down forests   homes   producing oil

3 Work in pairs. Say which things you do to help the environment.

- use public transport
- use energy-saving lights
- recycle
- buy local products

4 🔘 2.13 Listen to Veena talking about the environment. Which things in activity 3 does she mention?

5 🔘 2.13 Listen again and complete the table with no more than three words.

environmental problem	[1] people are not _____ enough
reasons	[2] people want to buy the _____ things
how we can help	[3] can use _____ again.
how Veena helps	gives things to [4] _____; sells them [5] _____; recycles things that aren't good

Living IELTS

SAYING YOU'RE NOT SURE

1 🔘 2.14 Listen and complete the sentences with these words.

> guess   think   sure

1 I _____ the main problem is not recycling enough.
2 I _____ people always want to buy the latest things …
3 I'm not _____.

2 🔘 2.14 Listen to the sentences again and practise.

6 Think of an environmental problem. Make notes about it. Think about …

- what it is.
- the reasons it is happening.
- how you prepare for it.
- what we can do to help.
- how you try to protect the environment.

7 Work in pairs. Take turns to talk about the topic card. Use the notes you made in activity 6 to help you.

> **Describe how you try to help the environment.**
>
> You should say:
> - what you think the biggest environmental problem is
> - what the reasons are for this
> - what we can do to help
> and explain how you try to protect the environment.

WRITING

PROBLEM-SOLUTION ESSAY

1 Work in groups. Decide on the three best ways we can protect the environment.

- [ ] recycling
- [ ] buying less
- [ ] flying less
- [ ] using less energy
- [ ] using public transport
- [ ] buying things locally
- [ ] stopping pollution
- [ ] writing to politicians

2 Read the question and underline the key words.

We are using up the world's resources too quickly. Describe three ways we can stop this.

3 Read the paragraph and tick the ideas in activity 1 it contains.

Today, people are putting themselves and many animals in great danger. We are using the world's resources too quickly and we are also polluting the environment. We need to do three things to stop this situation. First, we need to control the world's population. Second, we have to control pollution. Finally, everyone should try to use less energy. In this way, we can help to protect our world.

WRITING SKILLS

ORGANISING A PARAGRAPH (2)

4 Read the paragraph again and number the ideas in the order they are mentioned. Which three words does the writer use to introduce the three ways to solve the problem?

- [ ] why the problem exists
- [ ] conclusion
- [ ] three ways to solve the problem
- [ ] the problem

Bridge to IELTS

LISTING

Listing helps the reader understand your ideas. Tell the reader how many ideas you will write about. Then tell them which idea you are writing about.

5 Read the essay title. Make notes about your ideas in the table.

Animals are in great danger because of human activity. Describe three ways we can help them.

1 What is the problem?	
2 Why does the problem exist?	
3 Three ways to solve the problem	
4 Conclusion	

6 Write a short essay. Use the model in activity 3 and the notes you made in activity 5 to help you.

VOCABULARY

ADJECTIVES TO DESCRIBE OBJECTS

1 Work in pairs. Describe the car in the picture on page 95. Use the words below.

> exciting   modern   fast   safe
> light   cheap   efficient

2 Match the words in activity 1 with their opposites below.

> boring   dangerous   expensive   heavy
> inefficient   old-fashioned   slow

3 Complete the sentences with the adjectives in activities 1 and 2.

1 I don't like watching car racing – it's _____. I'm really not interested in it.
2 Computers inside modern cars can help to stop accidents. Today's cars are quite _____.
3 Electric car batteries are becoming more _____. You can drive a long way with them.
4 An electric car battery is quite _____ to recharge – it takes nearly 10 hours.
5 We can't buy this car because it's too _____ and we haven't got enough money.

4 Work in pairs. Describe your car or your family's car.

READING

1 Read the webpage and decide which kind of competition Supermileage is.

a	sports	**d**	art
b	business	**e**	other
c	engineering		

2 Read the webpage again and choose the correct answers.

1 The competition is for …
   a engineers.
   b cars.
   c engineering students.
2 The winning vehicle can travel …
   a more kilometres.
   b faster.
   c with more people.

The Supermileage Competition

The aim of Supermileage is to help engineering students improve their design and management skills.

Competition Aim

To design and build a long distance vehicle. The vehicle that travels longer on less fuel than the others is the winner.

3 Read the team blogs and match two of the headings with gaps 1 and 2.

A Race day **B** Team meeting **C** Design meeting

Brackley College Supermileage team

February [1] _____

It's very exciting – for our final year project we're entering the Supermileage competition in Michigan. We met for the first time today and gave our team members jobs. There are three people on each team. Our team leader is Khaled. He's more experienced at project management than Pat or me. Pat is the designer – she's better than the rest of us at using computers for design. And then there's me – the mechanic – I'm good at fixing things. Together, we're a good team, but can we win?

March [2] _____ _____

Today was an important meeting. We made some big decisions. At the last meeting we decided to make some of the car from fibreglass, but Khaled found a lighter material than fibreglass – carbon fibre – so we decided to use this. Then Pat changed the shape of the car to make it faster and safer. Finally, we chose our driver – Pat, she's smaller than the rest of us. Unfortunately, she's never driven a car before ...

Search [_____] **GO!**

About | Forum | Team Sites | Resources | Contact us

4 Read the blogs again and complete the summary. Use no more than three words in each gap.

Brackley Supermileage Team report

February: We chose [1] _____ for the team.

There are [2] _____ students in the team.

Khaled is our [3] _____; [4] _____ is the designer. Henri is the mechanic.

March: We changed the [5] _____ of the car to make it lighter. We also changed the car's [6] _____ to make it go faster.

5 Find words in the blogs which mean ...

1 work done over a period of time: p _ _ _ _ _ _
2 a person who plans and makes something: d _ _ _ _ _ _ _
3 a person who repairs machines: m _ _ _ _ _ _ _
4 a material made from plastic and glass: f _ _ _ _ _ _ _ _ _
5 a thin and strong material: c _ _ _ _ _ f _ _ _ _

GRAMMAR

COMPARATIVES

To compare two things you use a comparative adjective + *than*.

a **lighter** material **than** fibreglass

We form comparative adjectives by adding *-r* or *-er* to adjectives with one syllable.

safe – safer   fast – faster

With words ending vowel + consonant we double the consonant + *-er*.

big – bigger

With words ending with *-y* we add *-ier*.

friendly – friendlier

With longer adjectives we use *more* + adjective.

*He's **more experienced than** me.*

Some adjectives are irregular.

good – better   bad – worse   far – further

📓 **GRAMMAR REFERENCE PAGE 143**

1 Read the blogs in Reading activity 3 on page 95 again and find six comparative adjectives.

2 Complete the text with the correct form of the adjectives in brackets.

September test run

We tested our car today. We saw all the other cars too. The car from the Universite Normandin looks great – it looks ¹ _____ (good) than ours but it was ² _____ (expensive). At 30 kilos, it's ³ _____ (heavy) than ours. The Oakville University car driver is ⁴ _____ (bad) at driving than the other drivers, but she's ⁵ _____ (small) and ⁶ _____ (thin). I think our car's ⁷ _____ (light) and ⁸ _____ (fast) than the others. Now Pat's learnt to drive, I'm sure we can win!

3 Look at the information about the two cars and write sentences comparing them.

Brackley College	Universite Normandin
kilos: 28	kilos: 30
kilometres per hour: 15	kilometres per hour: 14
distance on one litre of fuel: 4 000 km	distance on one litre of fuel: 4 020 km
cost: $2 300	cost: $2 600

PRONUNCIATION

-er ENDINGS

1 💿 2.15 Listen and notice how you say *-er* in comparative adjectives.

2 Underline the /ə/ sound in the comparative adjectives.

It's lighter than this one.
It's faster than the others.
It's much cheaper than before.
It lasts longer than the others.

3 💿 2.16 Listen and practise the comparative adjectives.

READING

1 Work in pairs. Look at the pictures. Say what you know about these buildings and structures.

2 ⏱ **Read the passage in three minutes and match the paragraphs with the pictures in activity 1.**

THINK BIG
- the world's greatest engineering projects

At Construction Monthly UK, we like cool engineering and here's a list of the greatest engineering projects in the world. You may not agree with all of them, but everyone agrees that engineers think big!

1 The Millau Viaduct

It's the most beautiful modern bridge in the world and it's also the tallest at 245 metres high. It was built in France over three years. The bridge has eight parts and crosses the river Tarn. It has a dramatic shape but it doesn't have a big impact on the environment.

2 Burj Khalifa

The world's highest building was an easy choice for this list. The engineers broke every height record by 818 metres — over 300 metres taller than any other building. This incredible steel and glass tower in Dubai took just six years to build.

3 The Three Gorges Dam

China has built the world's largest hydroelectric power station on the Yangtze River. It is over two kilometres long and produces three per cent of China's electricity. This is enough electricity for Beijing for one year! The gigantic dam has increased electricity production and has also reduced flooding.

4 The Big Dig

It's the most expensive road project in American history — the Big Dig. The project is to move a road, which originally went through the middle of Boston, under the city through a tunnel. The final bill? $22 billion!

5 Large Hadron Collider

This machine is the biggest experiment on Earth. In a 27 km long tunnel just outside Geneva, Switzerland, scientists are trying to see how the universe looked at the beginning of time. The giant experiment includes the world's heaviest magnet at five metres wide and 25 metres long.

3 **Read the passage again and write YES, NO or NOT GIVEN.**

1 The Millau bridge has an interesting design. _____
2 The Burj Khalifa is in the middle of the business area. _____
3 Two per cent of Beijing's power comes from the dam. _____
4 The road in Boston went to New York. _____
5 Scientists are researching what happened at the start of the universe. _____

4 **Find the words in the passage and choose the correct meaning, a or b.**

1 *impact*
   a effect
   b difficulty

2 *tower*
   a a bridge to take cars across valleys
   b a tall straight building

3 *hydroelectric*
   a power from water
   b power from wind

4 *tunnel*
   a a road over a city
   b a road under the ground

5 *magnet*
   a iron that makes metal move towards it
   b a machine

GRAMMAR

SUPERLATIVES

To compare more than two things you use superlative adjectives. Superlative adjectives show the greatest quality.

*This machine is **the largest** experiment on earth.*

We form superlative adjectives with *the* and by adding *-st* or *-est* to adjectives with one syllable.

*wide – **the** wid**est***   *high – **the** high**est***

With words ending vowel + consonant we double the consonant + *-er*.

*big – the big**gest***

With words ending with *-y* we add *-iest*.

*heavy – the heav**iest***

With longer adjectives we use *the most* + adjective.

*beautiful – **the most** beautiful*

Some adjectives are irregular.

good – the best   *bad – the worst*

📖 **GRAMMAR REFERENCE PAGE 143**

1 Look back at the passage in Reading and find the superlative adjectives of these adjectives.

> great   beautiful   heavy   tall
> expensive   large

2 Complete the sentences with the superlative form of the adjectives below. Some sentences have more than one answer.

> long   tall   strong   ugly   bad

1 Before the Burj Khalifa, Taipei 101 was _____ building in the world.
2 Bridges have to be safe even in _____ winds.
3 That's a really terrible building, it's _____ I've seen.
4 The world's _____ underwater pipeline runs from Norway to Britain.
5 My _____ experience was at the top of the Eiffel Tower. I really don't like high places.

Discussion

Work in groups. Discuss the engineering projects in the unit, or another engineering project. Say which is the greatest and why.

Present your ideas to the other groups.

LISTENING

1 Work in pairs. Look at the pictures and match the old products with the new ones.

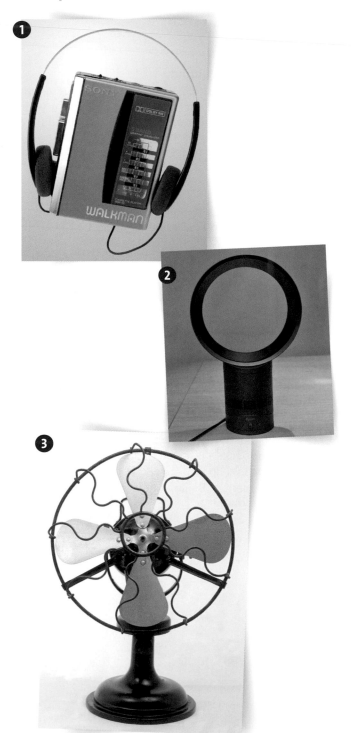

④

⑤

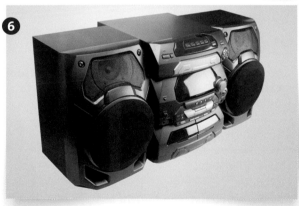

⑥

2 Work in pairs. Say which things in the pictures you have or you would like to have and why.

3 Tick three things in the list below that you think a design engineer does. Then work in pairs and discuss your answers.

1 thinks of new ideas ☐
2 researches products by other people ☐
3 uses new technology ☐
4 leads a team of people ☐
5 understands business ☐
6 helps to build the product ☐
7 draws designs ☐

4 🔘2.17 **Listen to the lecture and check your answers to activity 3.**

5 🔘2.17 **Listen again and choose the correct answers.**

1 Today design engineers work …
   a in the best companies.
   b in the best jobs in big companies.
   c in research departments.

2 Design engineers are good at …
   a working in different industries.
   b answering questions.
   c solving problems.

3 James Dyson designed a better …
   a CD player.
   b vacuum cleaner.
   c computer.

4 Naoto Fukasawa believes good design comes from …
   a experience.
   b nature.
   c a good education.

5 Jonathan Ive says success is because of …
   a good ideas.
   b teamwork.
   c good communication.

Discussion

Work in pairs. Decide what is the most important thing about a design. Think about …

- how it looks.
- how it works.
- how easy it is to use.
- how much it costs.

SPEAKING

MY FAVOURITE THING

1 **Work in pairs. Ask and answer the questions.**

1 What was the last thing you bought?
2 Where did you buy it?
3 What did you like about it? Think about …
- features
- design
- price
- quality
- usefulness

2 🔊 2.18 **Listen to three speakers talking about their favourite things that they bought recently. Complete the table.**

Speaker	What they bought	When they bought it	Where they bought it
Megumi	a smart phone	¹ _____	online
Caroline	² _____	last week	³ _____
Mohammed	⁴ _____	⁵ _____	in Singapore

3 🔊 2.18 **Listen again and complete the sentences.**

1 Megumi's phone is good _____. It has the same features as other phones and is _____.
2 Caroline wanted something _____ and thinks they look really stylish and _____.
3 Mohammed bought it because it's _____ and _____ than a mobile phone.

Living IELTS

TALKING ABOUT WHAT YOU LIKE

🔊 2.19 **Listen and complete the phrases for talking about what you like.**

1 I like it _____.
2 I love them _____.
3 I _____ like it.

4 **Think of your favourite thing. Make notes about it. Think about …**

- what it is.
- where you bought it.
- why you bought it.
- why you like it.

5 **Work in pairs. Take turns to talk about the topic card. Use the notes you made in activity 4 to help you.**

Describe your favourite object.

You should say:
- what it is
- where and when you bought it
- why you bought it
and explain why you like it.

WRITING

COMPARISON ESSAY

1 Work in pairs. Say what are the biggest building projects in your country.

2 Read the essay title and underline the key words.

> The map shows two cities: Mink and Deville. The cities need a new transport link. Choose the best form of transport.

3 Look at the map and complete the table.

	train [1] _____	motorway	road [2] _____
cost	$25 million	$20 million	$20 million
time to build	six years	two years	four years
journey time	[3] _____	60 minutes	[4] _____
people per journey	500 people	20 people	20 people

4 Read the essay. What does the student recommend to build?

> The table shows four choices for a new transport link. The left column shows the cost, time to build, journey time and number of people each one can carry.
>
> The train tunnel can carry the largest number of people. However, it is the most expensive choice and it also takes the longest time to build. The road bridge and the motorway cost the same. However, the journey is faster with the road bridge than the motorway.
>
> I think the road bridge is the best choice. It is quicker to build than the tunnel and it is the same price as the motorway.

WRITING SKILLS

FOR AND AGAINST

5 Read the essay again. Number these ideas in the order they appear in the essay.

   a conclusion: saying what the best choice is ☐
   b introduction: saying what the table shows ☐
   c main section: comparing the different choices ☐

6 Read the essay title. Underline the most important information in the table.

> The table shows the choices for Urbana's new urban transport system. Choose the best form of transport.

	tram	bus route	underground
cost	$15 million	$10 million	$10 million
time to build	three years	two years	eight years
journey time	50 minutes	1 hour 15 minutes	20 minutes
people per journey	100 people	20 people	500 people

Unit 12
Plans and predictions

READING

1 **Match the words with the pictures and say what each activity involves. Use these phrases.**

study abroad: in another country, university, study subject in English

internship: in a company, training, skills, earn money, get experience

gap year: travel, another country, learn about life

2 **Work in pairs. Look at the text and decide where it is from.**

a a magazine
b a web forum
c a chat room

3 (3min) **Read the text and match the people with the plans.**

1	Cindy	**a**	gap year
2	Jet	**b**	internship
3	Isabel and Jasmin	**c**	study abroad
4	Patrice	**d**	no plans yet

4 **Read the text again and choose the correct answers.**

1 Cindy is going to study ... in her free time.
  a electrical engineering
  b Japanese
  c flower arranging

2 Patrice is going to do an internship to …
  a make parts for cars.
  b stay near home.
  c make money.

3 Isabel and Jasmin are going to …
  a stay at home.
  b travel around Europe only.
  c see countries all over the world.

4 At the end, Jet …
  a knows what he wants to do.
  b decides to stay at home.
  c has to think about the choices.

Subject: Plans for after the course
Contributor

11 March 15.35	
Jet	Hi, guys. What are you going to do after the course? Are you going to stay at home like me? Or are you going to do something new? Give me some ideas!

11 March 15.40	
Cindy	I've chosen to go on a Study Abroad Year. I'm going to finish my first year exams here, then I'm going to study at a University in Tokyo for my second year. I'm going to study electrical engineering and Ikebana – flower arranging – in my spare time.

11 March 15.40	
Patrice	Wow, Tokyo. I'm not going to go far away. I'm going to do an internship – I'm going to work for an engineering company that makes electrical parts for cars. I can earn money and learn more about my subject. That's my plan.

11 March 16.40	
Isabel	Jet – get off your sofa and do something. Jasmin and I aren't going to stay at home like you. We're off on a gap year. We're making plans to travel around Europe for a month. Then we're off to Thailand and Vietnam for two months and then we're going to China and Australia. We're going to have lots of fun.

11 March 17.00	
Jet	Hey, thanks for the ideas. I feel like I have to do something too now. What's the best choice: Study Abroad Year; an internship or a gap year?

Vocabulary

Collocations

1 Match the verbs with the nouns. There may be more than one answer.

1	make	a	money
2	earn	b	an internship
3	do	c	fun
4	have	d	plans

2 Complete the collocations with the prepositions.

> at (x2)   for   about   around

1 study _____ university
2 work _____ a company
3 stay _____ home
4 learn _____ a subject
5 travel _____ a country

3 Match the phrases with *off* with the meanings.

1	far off	a	to go somewhere
2	we're off	b	to leave a bus or stand up from a chair
3	get off	c	a long way

4 Work in pairs. Say what you think is the best suggestion in the passage.

GRAMMAR

GOING TO

You use *going to* + verb to talk about your plans for the future.

I'**m going to** work with an engineering company.
I'**m not going to** go too far away.
Are you **going to** do something new?
What **are** you **going** to do after the course?

subject + *be* + (*not*) *going to* + verb

📖 GRAMMAR REFERENCE PAGE 143

1 Look at the passage again and underline the examples of *going to*.

2 Complete the sentences with the correct form of *going to*.

  1 It _____ be nice to see Cindy again.
  2 When _____ you _____ take the test?
  3 Who _____ go with you this evening?
  4 We _____ (not) see a film tonight, we're too tired.
  5 I _____ (not) visit my family this weekend.

3 Look at the pictures and complete the sentences about Jet's plans. Use *going to* and the verb in brackets.

  1 Jet _____ an internship. (apply for)
  2 He's _____ on September 14. (start)
  3 Jet's _____ for AU Engineering. (work)
  4 He's _____ on December 20. (finish)
  5 Then Jet's _____ a holiday in Turkey. (have)

4 Write questions for the other students.

  1 What / you / do / after / course?
  2 Where / you / study?
  3 How long / you / study for?

5 Work in groups of four. Student A, turn to page 125. Student B, turn to page 127. Student C, turn to page 125. Student D, turn to page 124. Read the information about your plans for after the course. Ask and answer the questions and complete the table below.

  Student A   Erik, what are you going to do after the course?
  Student B   I'm going to study abroad.

name	what	where	how long

LISTENING

1 **What are the benefits of doing a gap year? Tick the statements you agree with. Cross the statements you don't agree with.**

You have time to think about your future. ☐
You learn about different countries and cultures. ☐
You become more independent. ☐
You develop new skills ☐
You develop your confidence. ☐

2 **Work in pairs and discuss your answers to the questions in activity 1.**

3 🔘 2.20 **Listen to Izabela and Raoul talking about a gap year. Which of the ideas in activity 1 do they mention?**

4 🔘 2.20 **Listen again and choose Y (yes), N (no) or NG (not given).**

1 Izabela is going to spend her gap year travelling and working. Y / N / NG
2 She is going to spend time in Australia. Y / N / NG
3 Raoul thinks it may be difficult for her to return to education after her trip. Y / N / NG
4 They agree the trip is worthwhile. Y / N / NG

5 **Who has these opinions about the gap year? Write I for Izabela and R for Raoul.**

It's going to impress a future employer. ____
It's going to be very challenging. ____
It's going to be a good opportunity to travel at length. ____
It's going to be too expensive. ____
It's going to be a waste of time. ____

Discussion

Work in pairs. Discuss the question.

Would you like to do a gap year like Izabela? Why? / Why not?

PRONUNCIATION

GOING TO

1 🔘 2.21 **Listen to the two sentences and match them with the correct pronunciation.**

1 Are you going out this evening? /ɡəʊɪŋtə/
2 Is she going to do a gap year? /ɡəʊɪŋ/

2 🔘 2.22 **Listen to the six sentences. Write 1 if you hear / ɡəʊɪŋ / and write 2 for / ɡəʊɪŋtə /**

1 ____   4 ____
2 ____   5 ____
3 ____   6 ____

3 **Look at the audioscript on page 137 and practise saying the sentences.**

Reading

1 Work in pairs. Describe the pictures. Use these words.

education   online   learning   interactive

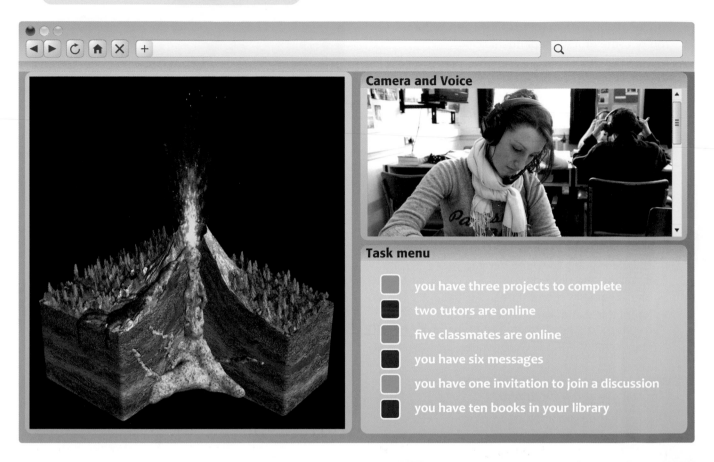

Camera and Voice

Task menu

- you have three projects to complete
- two tutors are online
- five classmates are online
- you have six messages
- you have one invitation to join a discussion
- you have ten books in your library

2 Read the passage and match the headings with the paragraphs. There are two extra headings.

1	the cost of education	Paragraph ___
2	education in 2020	Paragraph ___
3	learning times	Paragraph ___
4	places to learn	Paragraph ___
5	private education companies	Paragraph ___
6	learning equipment	Paragraph ___

Bridge to IELTS

MATCHING HEADINGS AND PARAGRAPHS

Making questions from the headings can help you find which paragraph the heading matches.
e.g. 2 education in 2020
What will education be like in 2020?
Make questions with the other headings and use the questions to help you find the paragraph in the passage.

Where's the classroom gone?

A What is traditional education? Today, it's a classroom, a teacher and a book. But will this be the same in 2020? The answer is almost certainly, 'No, it won't.' So, how will students learn in the future? Advances in technology will change where we learn and how we learn. Education will be available when and where it is needed, it will be more interactive, and it will be cheaper than it is now.

B Students won't use books in 2020; they will have a small digital tool to carry all the information they need. This tool will be a library, a mobile phone, a TV, a computer and a digital recorder. It won't have a keyboard –students will use their voice to use it.

C Learning won't start in the morning and finish in the afternoon; students will be able to study and learn 24 hours a day, seven days a week. Some work will be done alone, but a lot more will be done in pairs or in groups, and students will communicate with other students across the world to do projects.

3 Read the passage again and choose the correct answers.

1 Education will …
   a use advanced technology.
   b become cheaper.
   c take longer.

2 Students won't need to …
   a type.   **b** read.   **c** speak.

3 Students will study more often …
   a individually.
   b in lectures.
   c in pairs and small groups.

4 A … will watch the student's progress.
   a computer programme **b** tutor **c** parent

4 Find these words in the passage and match them with the meanings.

> virtual   interactive   digital   headset   keyboard   tool

1 something not real, made by a computer: _____
2 information that is in the form of 1s and 0s: _____
3 something usually held in your hand to help you do a job: _____
4 the part of your computer that you type with: _____
5 a piece of equipment you wear on your head which lets you hear, see and say things: _____
6 involving people communicating with each other: _____

D So what will happen to the teacher and the classroom? Well, we won't spend a lot of time in the classroom. Students will meet online and will have a group of teachers and experts to help them with their learning. A virtual tutor – or intelligent programme – will watch the student's progress and tell parents and teachers how they are doing. When a student doesn't understand something, the virtual tutor will help them. It will even be able to take students into a virtual world where they can experience situations for themselves. For example, if you are studying volcanoes, you will put on your headset and it will take you to a volcano to see what happens.

In the future, when we ask *Where's the classroom gone?* the answer will be *The classroom is all around us.*

GRAMMAR

WILL (NOT)

You use *will*, *will not* or *won't* to talk about what will happen in the future.

*Students **will** meet online.*
*We **won't** spend a lot of time in the classroom.*
*But **will** this be the same in 2020? Yes, it **will**. / No, it **won't**.*
*How **will** students learn?*

subject + *will* (*not* / *won't*) + verb

📖 **GRAMMAR REFERENCE PAGE 143**

1 Look at the text again and underline the examples of *will* and circle the examples of *won't*.

2 Complete the paragraph with *will* or *won't* and the verbs in brackets.

In 2020, education ¹ _____ (be) more like a business. The government ² _____ (not control) all our schools and universities. Instead, private companies ³ _____ (have) many more schools. The schools ⁴ _____ (work) like private companies. People ⁵ _____ (pay) to use their rooms, and schools will work with businesses to help students work in that business.

3 Write sentences about students in the future.

1 ✗ go to libraries
   Students won't go to libraries in 2020.
2 ✗ read books
3 ✓ have meetings online
4 ✗ take tests
5 ✓ do projects with students in other countries
6 ✓ pay more for education

Discussion

Work in pairs. Say which ideas in Grammar activity 3 you agree or disagree with.

SPEAKING

MY PLANS FOR THE FUTURE

1 **How do you feel about making plans? Which statement best describes you?**

☐ I really enjoy making plans.
☐ I never make plans. It's a waste of time!
☐ I don't like to plan too far ahead.
☐ I make plans but I often change them!

2 **Work in pairs and compare your answers. Do you feel the same way about making plans or are you very different?**

3 🔘 **2.23 Listen to Lucia talking about her plans and choose the correct answers.**

1 Lucia is going to study …
   a Business.
   b Software engineering.

2 She is going to go there …
   a this year.
   b next year.

3 She feels very …
   a nervous and worried.
   b excited.

4 It's important to her because …
   a she loves Sweden.
   b she is interested in studying this subject.

4 🔘 **2.23 Listen again and complete the sentences.**

1 I'm extremely _____ about it!
2 It's going to be an _____ learning experience.
3 I really can't _____!
4 I'm certainly going to make the most of the _____.

5 **Think of your plan for the future. Make notes about it. Think about …**

- what you're going to do.
- when you are going to do it.
- how you feel about it.
- why it is important to you.

Living IELTS

GIVING YOURSELF THINKING TIME

You can give yourself more time to think about what you are going to say next by using phrases like, *It's rather hard to say …* and *let me see …*

6 **Work in pairs. Take turns to talk about the topic card. Use the notes you made in activity 5 to help you.**

Describe a personal plan you have for the future.

You should say:
- what you're going to do
- when you're going to do it
- how you feel about it
and explain why it is important to you.

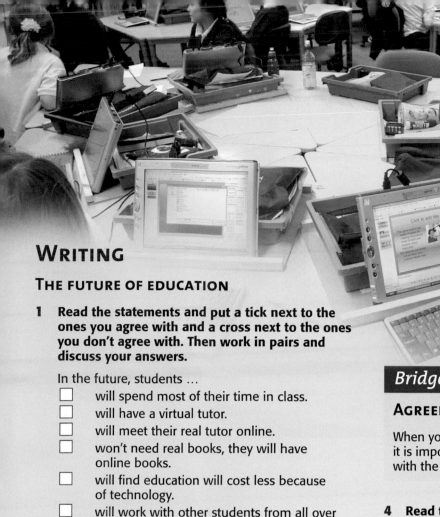

WRITING

THE FUTURE OF EDUCATION

1 Read the statements and put a tick next to the ones you agree with and a cross next to the ones you don't agree with. Then work in pairs and discuss your answers.

In the future, students …

☐ will spend most of their time in class.

☐ will have a virtual tutor.

☐ will meet their real tutor online.

☐ won't need real books, they will have online books.

☐ will find education will cost less because of technology.

☐ will work with other students from all over the world.

2 Read the question and underline the key words.

In the future, more students will be educated outside the classroom.
Do you agree or disagree with this statement?

3 Read the essay. Does the writer agree or disagree with the statement? Why? / Why not?

In my opinion, education in the future will not be very different from today. I think we will still have teachers in classrooms with students. We will have a lot more advanced technology like PCs in classrooms, but I don't agree that this will completely change the way we learn. I think the most important part of learning is the relationship between the teacher and the student. I don't believe this will change in the future.
Students will always need contact with their teacher and classmates. For this reason, I disagree with the statement.

Bridge to IELTS

AGREEING OR DISAGREEING

When you answer an essay that asks for your opinion, it is important to clearly say that you agree or disagree with the idea and why.

4 Read the essay again and choose the correct word to complete the sentence.

1 We *will / won't* have advanced technology in classrooms.

2 Advanced technology *will / won't* change the way we learn.

3 The student's relationship with the teacher *is / isn't* the most important thing.

4 Students *will / won't* need contact with their classmates.

WRITING SKILLS

GIVING YOUR OPINION

5 Read the essay again. Find three phrases for giving an opinion and two for (dis)agreeing. Which words follow (dis)agree?

6 Work in pairs. Make notes for the essay question. Use some of the ideas in activity 1 to help you.

In the future, technology will be the most important part of our education.
Do you agree or disagree with this statement?

7 Write a short essay about the question in activity 6. Use the model in activity 3 and the notes you made in activity 6 to help you.

1 Work in pairs. Student A, make questions using the words below. Student B, turn to page 127 and answer Student A's questions. Find five differences in the pictures.

1 food?   **A** Is there any food?   **B** Yes, there is.
2 litter?
3 music?   **A** Is there any music?
4 people? how many?
5 policemen? how many?
6 student helpers? how many?
7 posters? how many?
8 speakers? how many?
9 musicians? how many?

2 Complete the newspaper stories with the correct form of the adjectives in brackets.

New skyscraper complete

The world's ¹ _____ (tall) skyscraper has opened in Dubai. It's 300 metres ² _____ (big) than Taipei 101 and 450 metres ³ _____ (high) than New York's Empire State Building.

Marathon runner finishes

Lloyd Scott is the ⁴ _____ (slow) marathon runner in the world. He took six days to finish the race, much ⁵ _____ (late) than everyone else. Why? Because he wore the ⁶ _____ (heavy) running clothes – a diving suit.

3 Choose the correct verb form to complete the sentences.

Next year, for her Study Abroad Year, Halle ¹ *studies / is going to study* in Alexandria, Egypt. First she ² *is going to fly / flew* to Cairo, but she ³ *isn't going to stay / doesn't stay* there. She ⁴ *is going to travel / has travelled* straight to Alexandria to meet her friend Yuki. They ⁵ *are going to study / study* Arabic at the University of Alexandria.

4 Look at the graph and write sentences with *will* or *won't*.

become   continue   go   reach   be

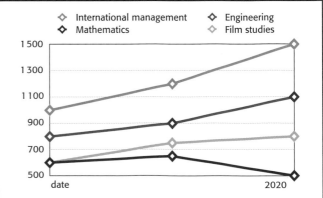

Number of students at the University by subject

◇ International management   ◇ Engineering
◆ Mathematics   ◇ Film studies

In 2020 the number of students at the University ¹ _will reach_ 5000. Let's look at this by subject. International management ² _____ to be the most popular subject. The number of engineering students will be over 1000 but ³ _____ above 1200. Unfortunately, mathematics ⁴ _____ very popular with only 500 students. However, other Arts subjects like film studies ⁵ _____ more popular.

VOCABULARY

1 Make nouns from these verbs.

1 direct _____   3 suggest _____
2 inform _____   4 educate _____

2 Make verbs from these nouns.

1 pollution _____   3 production _____
2 destruction _____   4 decision _____

3 Match the words with the definitions.

> expensive   dangerous   exciting
> inefficient   old-fashioned

1 something that costs a lot of money: _____
2 the opposite of *modern*: _____
3 a situation or something that can hurt you: _____
4 something that doesn't work very well: _____
5 not boring: _____

4 Complete the advert with these verbs.

> earn   have   make   do

> **WHAT ARE YOU GOING TO DO NEXT YEAR?**
>
> Why not ¹ _____ an internship? You can ² _____
> fun, meet new people and ³ _____ money. Don't
> wait till the end of the year - ⁴ _____ plans now.

SPEAKING TEST PREPARATION

1 Read the text and complete the table.

part	activity	time
1	introduction and ¹ _____	² _____ minutes
2	³ _____	3 minutes
3	⁴ _____	3–4 minutes

Speaking test

The speaking test has three parts: introduction
and interview, individual long turn and discussion.
Part one takes four to five minutes. The examiner
will ask you some general questions about
yourself. In part two, the examiner gives you a
task card. You have one minute to make notes
on the topic. Then you talk about the topic for
two minutes. The last part is a short discussion
with the examiner for three to four minutes. You
have practised all parts of the speaking test with
Bridge to IELTS.

**2 Work in pairs. Think of three ways you can
practise your speaking skills outside the class.**

Study Skills

REVISING VOCABULARY

**1 Work in pairs. Say how often and how you
revise vocabulary.**

**2 Read the passage and underline the ideas you
would like to try.**

Revising and remembering new vocabulary is
an important skill. A wide range of vocabulary is
tested in the IELTS examination. You can revise
anywhere and any time: at home, on the way to
college or at college. When your class finishes, go
over your notes and decide which words you need
to remember. Before the next class go over your
notes from the last class. At the end of the week,
make a list of words and test yourself or work with
a partner and test each other.

3 Choose a vocabulary set from the book.

**4 Divide the words into three groups. Use colours
to help you.**

a important words
b words I may need later
c words I only want to understand

5 Put the words from the groups into a table.

	I can remember this word.	Try again one week later.	I can remember this word.
extinct	✗	✓	✓

**6 Test yourself one week later. Did you remember
the word? Put a tick. Do you need to do more
revision? Put a cross and test yourself again at
the end of the week.**

Writing bank

1 HOME

WRITING AN EMAIL DESCRIBING ACCOMMODATION AND LOCAL AMENITIES (INFORMAL)

Mohammed is going to stay with Ben Fletcher's family in Cambridge in the UK. He wants to know about the accommodation and sends an email asking for information.

Email 🔍

Can you tell me about your house and the local area?

1 Read Mr Fletcher's reply and choose the correct answers.

Dear Mohammed

The house is small. There is a living room and there are three bedrooms. It is near the city centre. Near the house there is a swimming pool and there are some restaurants.

Best wishes

Ben Fletcher

1 The house is …
   a small.
   b medium-size.
   c big.

2 There are … bedrooms.
   a two
   b three
   c four

3 The house is … the city centre.
   a near
   b far from
   c in

4 There is a … near the house.
   a swimming pool
   b library
   c cafe

5 There are some … near the house.
   a offices
   b restaurants
   c shops

Ines is moving to Melbourne, Australia to live in Alice Connor's house.

Email 🔍

Dear Mrs Connor

Can you tell me about the room and the local area?

Ines

2 Look at Mrs Connor's notes and complete her email.

Room:
big / house in the city centre
bed ✓
bookshelves ✓
Local area:
park ✓
shops ✓

Dear Ines

The r___ is b___. There is a b___ and there are b___. The house is i___ the city centre. Near the house there is a p___ and there are some s___.

Regards

Alice Connor

Erika is moving to Cape Town in South Africa to live in Sanjita Malik's house.

Email 🔍

Dear Mrs Malik

Can you tell me about the room and the local area?

Erika

3 Look at Mrs Malik's notes and write an email reply from her to Erika.

Room:
medium-sized / near the city centre
TV set ✓
DVDs ✓
Local area:
museum ✓
shops ✓

Describing a room
There is a (sofa)
There are (some bookshelves)

Describing local amenities
There is a park
There are some shops

2 Festivals

Completing an online application form for a job (semi-formal)

The Edinburgh International Festival
9 August – 2 September

Are you good with people and free in August? If so, the beautiful city of Edinburgh wants you! We need volunteers to help visitors find their way around the city.

Please visit www.eifvolunteer.co.uk and complete the online application form.

1 Read the advertisement and choose the correct answers.

1 The festival is ... weeks long.
   a 2   **b** 3   **c** 4

2 They want ...
   a students only   **b** professionals only
   c anyone who is free in August.

3 They want people to ...
   a help tourists with directions.   **b** sell tickets.
   c help in theatres.

2 Rearrange the words to make questions.

a from / Where / you / are / ?
b do / What / do / you / ?
c is / name / What / your / ?
d your / are / interests / What / ?
e are / you / old / How / ?
f you / Are / female / male or / ?

3 Match a question in activity 2 with an answer below from the online application form.

EIF Volunteer	
1 Name:	Alfredo Foglia
2 Sex:	Male
3 Age:	22
4 Nationality:	Italian
5 Occupation:	student – tourism – Bologna University.
6 Likes:	music / sports (football☺!!).

Write a paragraph about yourself:

My name is Alfredo Foglia. I am a twenty-two-year-old Italian male. I study tourism at Bologna University. I like listening to music and playing sports. My favourite sport is football.

4 Read Rhonda's details and complete the paragraph about her.

EIF Volunteer	
1 Name:	Rhonda Hewson
2 Sex:	Female
3 Age:	19
4 Nationality:	American
5 Occupation:	student – business – Harvard University.
6 Likes:	travelling / meeting people (Brazil☺!!)

Write a paragraph about yourself:
My name is _____. I am a _____. I study _____ at _____. I like _____ and _____. My _____ country is _____.

5 Complete the notes with your details and write a paragraph about yourself.

EIF Volunteer
Name: _____
Sex: _____
Age: _____
Nationality: _____
Occupation: _____
Likes: _____

Write a paragraph about yourself:

_____
_____
_____
_____

Expressing likes and preferences
I **like** / **love** (meet**ing** new people).
I **enjoy** (play**ing**) sports.
My favourite band is Elbow.

Describing age
Compare
(1) *I am twenty years old. I am a German male.*
with
(2) *I am a twenty-year-old German male.*
In (2) the description of age is a compound adjective, so connect the words with '–' but drop 's' from 'years'.

Writing bank

3 TEAMWORK

COMPLETING AN EVALUATION FORM (SEMI-FORMAL)

1 **Choose the correct answer. The text is a/an:**

  a newspaper advertisement.
  b magazine article.
  c inter-office communication in a company.

Attention all managers

Please use the form below to help collect information on the performance of each of your workers.
Prepare your evaluations and opinions of each member of staff in a brief paragraph.

Give the person a mark from 0 to 4:

0 = terrible; 1 = poor/bad; 2 = average;
3 = good; 4 = excellent

Name: Lars Gunnerson

Appearance (smart? / untidy?)				
0	1	2	3 ✓	4

Punctuality (on time / late)				
0	1	2	3	4 ✓

Work performance (good / poor)				
0	1	2	3	4 ✓

Interaction with other workers				
0	1	2 ✓	3	4

Attendance (any time off?)				
0	1	2	3	4 ✓

Skills: speaks four languages
Opinion: ✓ ✓

2 **Read the notes on Lars and choose the correct answer in the evaluation paragraph.**

Lars [1] *usually / sometimes / never* looks smart. He [2] *usually / sometimes / never* arrives late. He [3] *usually / sometimes / never* works hard and he is [4] *friendly / unfriendly / nervous* although he can sometimes be shy. He [5] *often / sometimes / never* takes time off and he can speak four languages. I believe he is [6] *an excellent / an average / a below average* worker.

3 **Read the text again. Are the statements about Lars true or false?**

  a His appearance is usually good.
  b His work performance is good.
  c He is confident and talkative.
  d He sometimes doesn't come to work.
  e His manager has a high opinion of him.

4 **Read the notes on Akemi and complete her evaluation paragraph.**

Name: Akemi Kobayashi

Appearance (smart? / untidy?)				
0	1	2	3	4 ✓

Punctuality (on time / late)				
0	1	2	3	4 ✓

Work performance (good / poor)				
0	1	2 ✓	3	4

Interaction with other workers				
0 ✓	1	2	3	4

Attendance (any time off?)				
0	1	2	3	4 ✓

Skills: speaks five languages
Opinion: ✓ +

Akemi [1] _____ looks [2] _____ and she [3] _____ arrives on [4] _____. She [5] _____ works hard but she is [6] _____ and doesn't talk to many people. However, she [7] _____ takes time off and she [8] _____ speak five languages. In my [9] _____ she is a good [10] _____.

Describing appearance
She always looks smart.
He can sometimes be a little untidy.

Giving opinions
In my opinion …

Addition (*and*) **and contrast** (*but / However*)
*He arrives on time **and** works hard every day. (+/+)*
*He is friendly **but** he can sometimes be shy. (+/–)*
*She is shy. **However**, she never takes sick leave. (–/+)*

4 EDUCATION

LETTERS ASKING FOR AND REFUSING HELP (INFORMAL)

1 Read the letter. What type of letter is it?

   a a personal letter
   b a business letter
   c a letter of complaint

Dear Sue

How is my favourite aunt?
I hope you are well. I was wondering if you
could help me. There's a drama course in New
York I want to attend. It's a really good course
but it's very expensive – $10 000.
I only have $4 000!! You always say you want
to help me and I'm not working at the moment
so this is a great opportunity. Can you help?

With love
Layla xxx

2 Answer the questions.

   a Where does Layla want to go?
   b What does she want to do there?
   c What is the total cost of the course?
   d How much can Layla pay?
   e What does she want Sue to do?

3 Read Sue's reply. Can she help?

Dear Layla

1 It's really nice to hear from you.

2 Your drama course sounds great, but can
you pay for food and accommodation in New
York?

3 I'm afraid I can't help you with the $6 000.
I wish I could help you.

4 Why don't you get a job and save some
money?

Good luck – I hope you get to New York!

5 Lots of love
Sue

4 Order the stages of Sue's letter, 1–5:

   a Refuse to help   ____
   b Suggest other options   ____
   c Opening greeting   _1_
   d Closing salutation   ____
   e Discuss Layla's request   ____

5 Complete James's letter to his uncle.

[1] _____ Uncle Albert

I [2] _____ you are well.

I have the opportunity to study marine
biology in Australia, but they want $4 500.
I was [3] _____ if you [4] _____ help me.

Love and best wishes

James

6 Re-order the words in each line to reveal Uncle Albert's reply.

James / dear
hear / good / you / it's / from / to / .
biology course / fantastic / sounds / but / the
afraid / the money / have / I / don't / I'm / .
you / could / I / help / wish / I / .
speak / don't / parents / why / your / you / to / ?
you / I / get / Australia / hope / to / .
wishes / best / love / and
Albert

Asking for help
I was wondering if you could help me.

Refusing to help
I wish I could help you.

Apologising
I'm afraid …

Making suggestions
Why don't you (speak to your parents)?

Writing bank

5 BUILDINGS AND CITIES

WRITING A LETTER OF COMPLAINT (SEMI-FORMAL)

1 Read the text and choose the correct answer. The text is a/an:

  a advertisement.

  b newspaper article.

  c note to a friend.

Room to let
Large house. Share with five others.
Central location.
5 minutes walk from railway station.
Would suit young professional person.
Contact: S. Sawicki on 0129 229 992

2 Read the text. Are the statements true of false?

  a Six people usually share the house.

  b The house is in the city centre.

  c The room is good for a student.

3 Six months ago, John answered the advertisement and moved into the house. He has a problem. Read his letter to the landlord and tick (✓) John's problem.

  a His landlord wants too much money. ☐

  b Someone in the house is making too much noise. ☐

Email 🔍

Dear Mr Sawicki

I hope you and your family enjoyed your holiday last month.

I am writing in connection with one of the other people in the house, Dana Flynn.

The issue is that Dana and her friends make a lot of noise late at night.

I would appreciate it if you could ask her to be quiet after 10pm during the week.

Yours sincerely

John Henman

---

4 Read John's letter again. Number 1–6 the following stages in the order John does them.

  a He gives the reason for writing the letter. ____

  b He closes his letter with a semi-formal salutation and adds his full name. ____

  c He suggests a solution ____

  d He opens with a semi-formal salutation and a personal, friendly comment. _1_

  e He describes the problem. ____

5 Lisa Khalid lives in an apartment owned by Tom Smith. She wants to write to her landlord and tell him about a problem. Read her notes and complete her letter.

Reason: the neighbour, Mrs Alma
Problem: she doesn't cover her rubbish – it smells bad!
Solution: ask Mr Smith to speak to Mrs Alma

Dear Mr Smith
I hope you and your family are well.
I am writing _____
_____
_____
_____
_____
_____
_____
_____
_____
_____

Opening a semi-formal letter
Dear Mr / Ms / Mrs Smith,

Giving the reason for writing
I am writing in connection with … (+ noun)

Describing the problem
The issue is that … (+ verb / noun)

Suggesting a solution
I would appreciate it if you could … (+ verb)

Closing a semi-formal letter
Yours sincerely
(Lisa Khalid)

6 WORK

WRITING A LETTER THANKING A FRIEND (INFORMAL)

1 Read the text and choose the correct answer. The text is a/an:

a an advertisement.

b newspaper article.

c email to a friend.

> Hi Jack
>
> Are you okay? How is everything? Call me and let me know how you're doing.
> All the best
> Yves

2 Read Yves' reply and choose the correct answers.

a Yves was *at / away* from home last week.

b Yves and Jack *did some business / went on holiday* together.

c They had a *good / bad* time.

d *Kelly / Sabine* is Yves' wife.

e In his letter, Jack invites Yves for *another holiday / the weekend*.

Email	🔍

> Dear Yves
>
> How are you? I'm sorry for not writing sooner, but I was away on business all last week. I only got back last night.
>
> Thanks so much for the holiday. We had a fantastic time and didn't want it to end. Kelly and I really loved the boat trip around the island.
>
> Why don't you and Sabine come to our place and stay for the weekend? Any weekend in the next three months is good for us.
>
> I'm looking forward to hearing from you.
>
> Best wishes
> Jack

3 Read Ruby and Sam's emails and complete Ruby's letter.

> Sam
>
> I'm coming home today. My mother's feeling better now.
> I want to write and thank Carla for her beautiful present – I love it!
> Can I invite her to our place next weekend?
> R x

> Hi Ruby
>
> I'm happy you're coming home. I missed you. Good news about your mum. We're free next weekend so invite Carla. See you later.
> S x

> 1 _____ Carla
>
> 2 _____ are you? I'm 3 _____ for not writing sooner, but I was at 4 _____ all last week. She was ill but she's OK now.
>
> Thanks so much for the 5 _____. It was exactly what I wanted! The colours are beautiful.
>
> Why don't you 6 _____ to our place next weekend? We'd love to see you.
>
> I'm 7 _____ forward to hearing from you.
>
> Best 8 _____
> Ruby

4 Read the update. Then write a letter from Carla thanking Ruby and Sam for the weekend.

> Carla stayed for the weekend with Ruby and Sam. They went for a long walk by the sea. Carla loved it. After the weekend Carla had an accident and broke her leg. She spent two weeks in hospital.

- Open with their (first) names and an informal salutation.
- Apologise for not writing earlier – tell them what happened and say how long you were away for.
- Thank them for the weekend – say one thing you really liked about it.
- Invite them to your house in the mountains for a holiday.
- Close your letter with an informal salutation and your (first) name.

Opening an informal letter
Dear Irma / Kim / David

Apologising
I'm sorry for not writing sooner, but …

Thanking
Thanks (so much) for having us

Inviting
Why don't you (come and stay with us)?

Closing an informal letter
Best wishes

Writing bank

7 URBAN SPORTS

DESCRIBING STATISTICS IN A BAR CHART (ACADEMIC)

1 **Look at the chart and the description. Where would you expect to see it?**

a in a fashion magazine

b in an academic journal

c in a newspaper

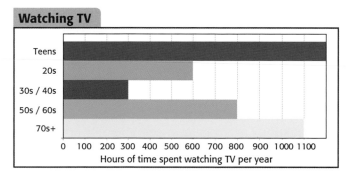

Watching TV

Hours of time spent watching TV per year

1 The bar chart shows how much time people in different age groups spend watching TV.

2 According to the figures, teenagers spend 1 200 hours a year watching TV. People in their twenties spend just 600 hours a year watching TV. Thirty and forty year olds spend just 300 hours, while fifty and sixty year olds spend 800 hours a year. People of seventy and above spend 1 000 hours a year watching TV.

3 In conclusion, we can see that teenagers and retired people spend more time watching TV than people of working age.

2 **Match a paragraph in activity 1 with a description below.**

a It's a conclusion. It sums up the trends based on the facts presented. ___

b It's an introduction. It gives us a description of the main idea. ___

c It's a summary of the facts. It gives us a description of the statistics. ___

3 **Are the statements true or false?**

a The first paragraph gives a specific, detailed description.

b The second paragraph gives a specific, detailed description.

c The writer of the text presents his/her opinion of the statistics in the main paragraph.

d In the main paragraph, the writer presents the facts illustrated in the bar chart.

e The last paragraph summarises the main trends presented in the data.

4 **Rearrange the sentences. When rewriting, add commas and full stops.**

a men and women / spend / their money / shows how / The chart

b the figures / on gadgets / spend £1 500 / a year / According to / men

c Women / while men / spend £50 / spend much more / a year

d can see / In conclusion / on gadgets / than women / we / that men / spend more

5 **Look at the bar chart. Complete the text with the correct phrases and statistics. Use the text in activity 1 to help you.**

Group sport

Hours of time spent doing group sport per year

_____ _____ _____ _____ how much time people in different age groups spend doing group sports.

_____ _____ _____ _____, teenagers spend _____ hours a year doing group sports. People in their twenties spend just _____ _____ _____ doing group sports. Thirty and forty year olds _____ _____ _____ _____, while fifty and sixty year olds _____ _____ _____ _____ _____. People of seventy and above _____ _____ any time doing group sports.

6 **Complete the conclusion with a, b or c.**

In conclusion, we can see that _____.

a ... young people do lots of group sport.

b ... old people don't do any group sport.

c ... as people get older, they do less group sport.

Presenting statistics

The chart / table shows ...

According to the figures,

In conclusion,

*30 year olds spend 300 hours, **while** 50 year olds spend 800 hours a year.*

8 THE NATURAL WORLD

DESCRIBING WHAT IS HAPPENING IN A GRAPH (ACADEMIC)

1 Look at the graph and read the text. What conclusions can you draw?

  a The rate of deforestation is going up.
  b The rate of deforestation is going down.
  c There is no change in the rate of deforestation.

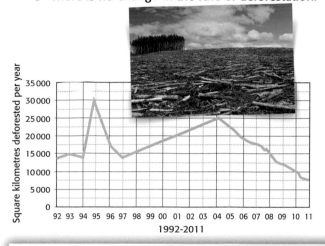

> The graph shows how much of the Brazilian rainforest was cut down over a 19-year period.
>
> According to the figures, the amount of deforestation stayed the same, at a rate of around 14000 square kilometres a year, between 1992 and 1994. Then there was a sharp increase in 1995. Almost 30000 square kilometres of rainforest was cut down. In 1996 and 1997 the rate dropped to around 14000 square kilometres a year but then rose gradually to 25000 square kilometres a year in 2004. From 2004 until 2011 there was a steady decline in deforestation to 750 square kilometres a year.

2 Read the text again. Match the beginnings and endings of the sentences.

1	Until '94 the rate remained	a	declined.
2	In 1995, deforestation rose	b	constant.
3	In 1996, the rate of deforestation	c	steadily.
4	From 1997 deforestation grew	d	decrease.
5	From 2004 there was a gradual	e	sharply.

3 Replace the words in italics with words that mean the same. Use the Key Vocabulary box to help you.

  a In 2011 there was a sharp *increase*.
  b Since August there has been a *steady fall*.
  c Prices *increased* sharply in April.
  d The number of tourists *decreased* last year.
  e Production rose *gradually* in 2012.
  f Interest rates *stayed the same* in October.

4 Describes what is happening in each graph.

  Example: *1. to remain constant*

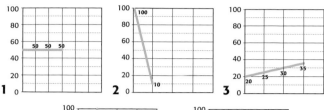

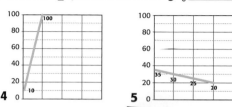

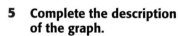

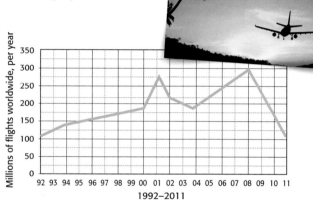

5 Complete the description of the graph.

The _____ shows how many holiday flights there were across the world over a 19-year period.
According _____ _____ _____, the number of flights _____ _____ from 100 million in 1992 to 175 million in 2000. Then there was a _____ _____ in 2001, to 260 million. That figure _____ to around 225 million in 2002. It continued to _____ until 2004, reaching 180 million. But then the number of flights started to _____ again. The number _____ _____ to nearly 300 million in 2008 and then _____ once again. It _____ _____ back to 100 million 2011.

> **Going up** ↑
> *increase / rise* (verb / noun)
>
> **Going down** ↓
> *decrease / fall / drop / decline* (verb / noun)
>
> **No change** →
> *stay the same / remain constant* (verb)
>
> | **adjectives** | **adverbs** |
> |---|---|
> | a **sharp** increase | to increase **sharply** |
> | a **gradual** rise | to rise **gradually** |
> | a **steady** decline | to decline **steadily** |

9 FAMILY

COMPARING TWO SETS OF STATISTICS (ACADEMIC)

1 Look at the diagram and read the text comparing life in the UK in 1971 with 2011. Which sentence best summarises the findings?

a Everything is different.

b Everything is the same.

c Some things are different but most are the same.

d Most things are different but some are the same.

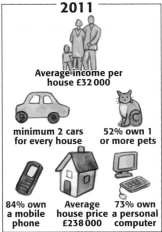

The diagram shows the changes in people's lives in the UK between 1971 and 2011.

In 1971 there was a maximum of one car to each house, while there were at least two cars per house and sometimes more in 2011. The average income per house in 1971 was £2 500. By contrast, the average income per house in 2011 was £32 000. The average house price was £238 000 in 2011, compared to just £5 600 in 1971. No one owned a mobile phone or computer in 1971, whereas in 2011 84% of people owned a mobile phone and 73% owned a personal computer. The only thing that didn't change was the number of pets people owned. 52% of people had one or more pets in 1971 and 52% had one or more in 2011.

2 Choose the correct answers.

a In 2011 some people had two cars, *while / and* it was usually one in 1971.

b The average salary was £2 500 in 1971, *by contrast / compared to* £32 000 in 2011.

c People paid £5 600 for a house in 1971, *compared to / whereas* they paid £238 000 in 2011.

d No one owned a mobile phone in 1971. *Whereas / By contrast*, 84% owned one in 2011.

e In 2011, 73% of the population owned a personal computer, *compared to / whereas* 0% in 1971.

f Half the population owned a pet in 1971 *while / and* the same amount owned one in 2011.

3 Complete the description of the diagram comparing life in Toronto in 1981 with 2011.

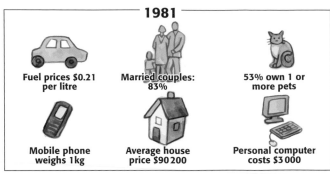

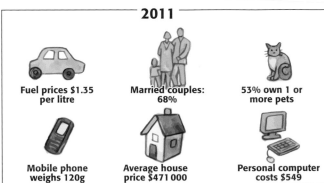

The diagram shows the changes in people's lives in Toronto between 1981 and 2011.

In 1981 fuel prices were $0.21 per litre, while
1 _____.

83% of couples were married in 1981. By contrast,
2 _____.

Mobile phones weighed just 120g in 2011, compared to 3 _____.
And a personal computer cost $3 000 in 1981, whereas 4 _____.
The only thing that didn't change was the number of pets people owned. 53% of people had one or more pets in 1981 and 5 _____.

Comparing and contrasting

Fuel was cheap in 1975. **By contrast**, *it was very expensive in 2011.*

76% of couples were married in 1998, **compared to** *64% in 2012.*

20% of people owned a mobile phone in 2000, **whereas** *80% of people owned one by 2010.*

In 1993, mobile phones were large and heavy, **while** *in 2005 they were small and light.*

52% of people owned pets in 1980 **and** *52% of people owned pets in 2000.*

10 CONSERVATION

DESCRIBING NUMBERS IN A PIE CHART (ACADEMIC)

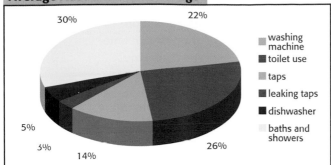

Average Australian Water Usage

- washing machine
- toilet use
- taps
- leaking taps
- dishwasher
- baths and showers

The chart shows how water is used in an average Australian home. Nearly a third of all the water in one house is used for bathing. Just over a quarter is flushed away down the toilet, while just under a quarter is used for washing clothes. 14% is used when turning the taps on and off in the bathrooms and kitchen. 5% is used by the dishwasher and 3% is wasted through leaking taps.

1 Look at the pie chart and read the text. Complete the sentence using the words in the box. Where in the text would you put this sentence?

> leaking taps   washing dishes   toilet use
> washing clothes   bathing

¹ _____, ² _____ and ³ _____ account for just over three quarters of the total water usage in an average Australian home.

2 Rearrange the words.

a used / 30% / bathing / of water / for / is
b is / of water / away / 26% / flushed
c the taps / of water / comes / 14% / out of
d used / dishwasher / of / water / 5% / is / in the
e is / of / wasted / 3% / water

3 Write a percentage from the box next to each phrase.

> 19%   21%   25%   26%   30%
> 34%   48%   50%   66%   69%

a nearly a third = _____
b just over a quarter = _____
c just under a half = _____
d more than two thirds = _____
e nearly a fifth = _____

4 The pie chart shows how energy is used in an average UK home. Use the data from the chart to make seven sentences, using the phrases below.

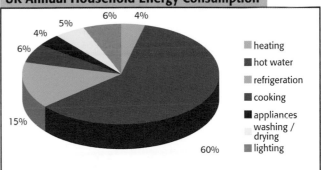

UK Annual Household Energy Consumption

- heating
- hot water
- refrigeration
- cooking
- appliances
- washing / drying
- lighting

Use these phrases:

4%		for lights on dark winter nights.
5%		to heat up food at mealtimes.
6%		to keep the house warm.
Just under a sixth	is used	on TVs and computers.
		to keep food cold.
Nearly two thirds		for the laundry.
		to heat up water for showers, baths and washing-up.

Connect some of your sentences. Use these linking words:

6% is used for refrigeration	**and**	6% is used for washing.
Nearly two thirds is used on heating the house,	**whereas** **while** **compared to**	just under a sixth is used to heat water.

Complete the description of the pie chart. Start by describing the largest segment.

The chart shows how energy is used in an average UK home. _____
_____
_____
_____

> **Describing numbers**
> *(Just under / over) two thirds is used on heating.*
> *A quarter is flushed away.*
> *More than half of all plastics are recycled.*
> *19% of food is wasted.*
> *20 billion kilos of bananas are eaten every year.*

Writing bank

11 DESIGN

COMPARING DATA IN A TABLE (ACADEMIC)

1 Look at the table and read the text comparing three mobile phones. Which summary best describes the information in the table?

a The lightest mobile phone is the best.
b The heaviest mobile phone is the best.
c Each mobile phone has advantages and disadvantages.

	Sanzen ST46	Raspberry 8-47	Pear UYE21
Battery (hours of talk time)	6.5	5.5	7
Weight (in grams)	114	99	135
Camera (megapixels)	8	5	11

The table shows data about three new designs of mobile phone.
The table compares the three models in terms of battery life, weight and camera resolution. It is clear that the heavier phones have a greater capability. The heaviest phone is the *Pear UYE21*, which weighs 135g. It also has the longest battery talk time, seven hours, and its camera has the highest resolution, 11 megapixels. The *Sanzen ST46* is lighter than the Pear, at 114g but the lightest mobile is the *Raspberry 8-47*, at 99g. However, the Raspberry's camera has the lowest resolution, 5 megapixels, and the shortest battery talk time, 5.5 hours.

2 Match questions 1-3 with answers a-c.

1 What does the table show?
2 What does the table compare?
3 What general pattern do you notice?

a The heavier phones have a greater capability.
b Data about three new mobile phones.
c The three models in terms of battery life, weight and camera resolution.

3 Answer the questions.

a Which is the heaviest mobile phone?
b How much does the heaviest phone weigh?
c Which phone has the longest talk time?
d How long does its battery last?
e Which camera has the highest resolution?
f How high is the highest resolution?

4 Write the questions. Then write full answers.

a lightest / mobile phone?
b how much / lightest / weigh?
c camera / lowest resolution?
d how high / lowest resolution?
e battery offers / shortest talk time?
f how long / shortest talk time?

5 You are going to write a comparison. Look at the table and complete the paragraphs.

	Aircoach LZ2	Jetstar X440	Gallant F-290
Passengers (capacity)	555	420	340
Weight (in tonnes)	650	505	290
Noise level 1 = quietest 20 = loudest	8	16	17

The table shows data about three new designs of _____.
The table compares the three models in terms of _____. It is clear that _____.

Now write a detailed comparison. Answer these questions to help you:

- Which plane can carry the most / the fewest passengers?
- Which is the heaviest / the lightest plane?
- Which is the loudest / the quietest plane?

Comparing figures
The highest / heaviest / noisiest
The lowest / lightest / quietest
It has / doesn't have as much ...

Contrasting
The Raspberry is the lightest. **However,** *it has the shortest battery life.*
The Gallant can carry 340 passengers, **while /**
whereas *the Aircoach can carry 555.*

12 PLANS AND PREDICTIONS

DESCRIBING PROPOSED CHANGES IN A DIAGRAM (ACADEMIC)

1 **Look at the plans. Is the statement below about proposed changes true or false?**

The living areas will be more open.

PRESENT LAYOUT   **PROPOSED LAYOUT**

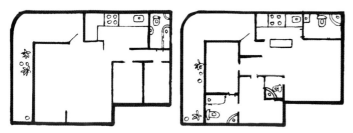

1 The first picture shows the present layout of an apartment and the second shows some proposed changes to the layout of the apartment.

2 The proposed changes will provide a much bigger open-plan living area and use existing rooms for different purposes.

3 At present, the bedrooms are near the entrance and there is a bathroom next to the kitchen. The dining room and living room area is quite small.

4 However, the plan is to remove the walls between the bedrooms and change the layout of the bathroom next to the kitchen. In place of the bedrooms there will be a bigger open living / dining area and a bigger kitchen. The dining room and the living room will both become bedrooms, but won't have en suite bathrooms.

2 **Read the text and match paragraphs 1–4 with statements a–d below.**

a It gives us specific details of the changes. _4_

b It gives us general details of the changes. ___

c It gives us specific details of what the apartment looks like now. ___

d It tells us what each picture shows. ___

3 **Complete the description of some proposed changes to a house with the words in the box.**

> place   present   utility   plan   en suite
> open-plan   extension

At ¹_____, there are three bedrooms and two bathrooms in the house. However, the ²_____ is to build an ³_____. This will provide two more bedrooms, both with ⁴_____ bathrooms. In ⁵_____ of two separate rooms, we will have a large, ⁶_____ kitchen / dining area. We will also add a ⁷_____ room for washing and drying clothes.

4 **Look at the pictures of the proposed changes to the apartment and tick (✓) the NOW or FUTURE column of the table.**

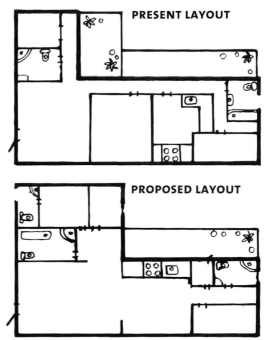

	NOW	FUTURE
A bedroom with en suite bathroom		✓
Bedrooms at opposite ends	✓	
Separate kitchen and dining room		
A bigger living room		
A utility room		
An extension		
3 bathrooms		
An office		
An open-plan kitchen / dining area		

5 **Follow the style of the text in Exercise 1 and write your own description for the pictures above.**

Describing proposed changes to a building
At present,
However, the plan is to …
In place of the (kitchen), there will be an (office).

Describing rooms and spaces
an en suite bathroom
a utility room (for washing and drying clothes)
an open-plan living / dining room
an extension (add extra rooms to an apartment)

Assignments

UNIT 2 Festivals
Student A

Read about the Festival of Colour.

The Festival of Colour is one of the largest festivals in India. It takes place in March. It's a fun day when people throw paint and coloured water on each other!

UNIT 5 Buildings and cities
Student A

Read the notes about the Ostankino Tower.
Use the information to make sentences. Then tell Student B about it.

The Ostankino Tower
in Moscow
they / start to build / in 1963
540 metres high – the third tallest building in the world
they / use / concrete
they / complete / four years

UNIT 6 Work
Student A

Ask and answer the questions you wrote in activity 5.
Read the notes about a job. Answer Student B's questions.
Then ask Student B questions about a different job.

What: bar tender
Where: restaurant
When: two years ago
How long: six weeks
What: take orders and prepare drinks

UNIT 7 Urban sports
Student A

Tell Student B about this sport or game. Student B decides which sport or game it is. Then guess Student B's sport or game.

- two players   *You need two players.*
- a quiet place
- to be fast
- to be very clever
- a board and pieces

Answer: chess

UNIT 8 The natural world
Student A

Read the information about a lake and answer Student B's questions.
Then ask Student B questions.

Lake Biwa is the biggest lake in Japan. It is famous for its beauty. However, over the past few years it has become smaller in size and has become polluted by industrial waste.

UNIT 12 Plans and predictions
This is the information about you. Take turns asking questions and answering the other student's questions.

Student C _____

travel
America
two months

what	where	how long
travel	America	two months

UNIT 12 Plans and predictions
This is the information about you. Take turns asking questions and answering the other student's questions.

Student D _____

exchange programme
University of Glasgow
six months

what	where	how long
exchange programme	University of Glasgow	six months

UNIT 9 FAMILY
STUDENT A

Read the information about a coming of age ceremony in the Guizhou region of China.

The Yi or Nuosu people live in the Guizhou region of China. Children become adults when they are seventeen years old. During the ceremony they take off their skirts and put on an adult skirt. This marks their coming of age.

UNIT 10 CONSERVATION (PAGE 87)
STUDENT A

1 Write questions. Then ask Student B the questions and write the answers.

   1 be / there / anywhere to have a party?
   2 we / have / student helpers?
   3 be / there / posters?

2 Write answers for Student B. Then answer Student B's questions.

   4 ✓ be / three bands
   5 ✓ we / have / three speakers
   6 ✗ there / not be / food

UNIT 10 CONSERVATION (PAGE 89)
STUDENT A

Write questions with *How much* or *How many*. Ask Student B your questions.

   1 How / water on earth is saltwater?
   2 How / people / not have clean water?
   3 How / water is in a human body?

Answer Student B's questions.

   a less than 1%
   b about 75%
   c 2400 litres

UNIT 3 TEAMWORK
Count your score: A = 1 point, B = 2 points, C = 3 points.

12–15 points
You're not very confident! Don't be so shy. Try to meet people and be more talkative.

9–12 points
You're quite confident. Be a little more friendly and you can really enjoy any new situation.

5–9 points
You like people and other people usually like you too. You're very confident.

UNIT 12 PLANS AND PREDICTIONS
This is the information about you. Take turns asking questions and answering the other student's questions.

Student A _____

study abroad
University of Montreal
six months

what	where	how long
study abroad	University of Montreal	six months

UNIT 10 CONSERVATION (PAGE 92)

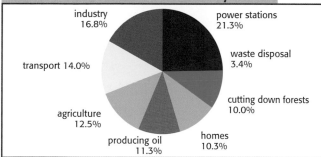

Annual Greenhouse Gas Emissions by Sector

industry 16.8%
power stations 21.3%
transport 14.0%
waste disposal 3.4%
agriculture 12.5%
cutting down forests 10.0%
producing oil 11.3%
homes 10.3%

Assignments

UNIT 2 FESTIVALS
STUDENT B

Read about the Water Festival.

The Water Festival celebrates the New Year in Thailand. It takes place in April and usually lasts for three days. People spend time throwing water on each other. No one is safe!

REVIEW UNITS 1 & 2
STUDENT B

Answer Student A's questions.

UNIT 5 BUILDINGS AND CITIES
STUDENT B

Read the notes about the Khalifa Tower.
Use the information to make sentences. Then tell student A about it.

The Khalifa Tower
in Dubai
they / start to build / in 2004
828 metres high – the tallest building in the world
they / use / concrete
they / complete / six years

UNIT 6 WORK
STUDENT B

Ask and answer the questions you wrote in activity 5. Read the notes about a job. Answer Student A's questions. Then ask Student A questions about a different job.

What: attendant
Where cinema
When: last summer
How long: two months
What: check tickets and give information

REVIEW UNITS 5 & 6

STUDENT B

Answer Student A's questions.

1 Name: CN Tower
2 City: Toronto, Canada
3 Builder: Canadian National Railway
4 Date: 1976
5 Materials: concrete and glass
6 Why special: It is a symbol of the city. It is the world's tallest tower (*Guiness World Records 2010*).

UNIT 7 URBAN SPORTS
STUDENT B

Tell Student A about this sport or game. Student A decides which sport or game it is. Then guess Student A's sport or game.

- a team of players *You need a team of players.*
- to be good at teamwork
- to be fast
- to be very strong
- to be good at kicking the ball

Answer: rugby

UNIT 8 THE NATURAL WORLD
STUDENT B

Read the information about a river and answer Student A's questions. Then ask Student A questions.

> The River Nile is in Egypt and the longest river in the world. It is famous for the amazing views along its banks. However, over the past few years many hotels, shops and restaurants on the banks have closed because big boats have food and souvenirs on board for tourists.

UNIT 9 FAMILY
STUDENT B

Read the information about the coming of age ceremony in the Yunnan region of China.

> The Pumi people live in Yunnan region of China. Children become adults when they are thirteen years old. They step first on a piece of fat with their right foot and then step on a bag of rice with their left foot. This marks their coming of age.

UNIT 10 CONSERVATION (PAGE 87)
STUDENT B

1 Write answers for Student A. Then answer Student A's questions.

1 ✓ the Student's Union
2 ✗ we / not / have / student helpers
3 ✗ there / not / be / any posters

2 Write questions. Then ask Student A the questions and write the answers.

4 we / have / music?
5 be / there / speakers?
6 be / there / food?

UNIT 10 CONSERVATION (PAGE 89)
STUDENT B

Write questions with *How much* or *How many*. Ask Student A your questions.

1 How / fresh water is drinkable?
2 How / water is in the north and south poles?
3 How / water is used to make one burger?

Answer Student A's questions.

a 97.5%
b 1.1 billion
c about 40 litres

REVIEW UNITS 10, 11 & 12
STUDENT B

UNIT 12 PLANS AND PREDICTIONS
This is the information about you. Take turns asking questions and answering the other student's questions.

Student B _____

internship
PC Computers, France
three months

what	where	how long
internship	PC Computers, France	three months

Audioscripts

UNIT 1

Track 1.1
Ana: Hello, Sergei!
Sergei: Hi, Ana! How are you?
Ana: I'm fine, thanks. And you?
Sergei: I'm very well, thanks.
Ana: Sergei, this is Eva. She's from Argentina.
Eva: Hello, Sergei. Nice to meet you.
Sergei: Nice to meet you too! I'm from Russia.
Eva: Are you a new student?
Sergei: Yes, I am.
Eva: I'm a new student too!

Track 1.2
Fouad: Hello. I'm a new student. I'm here for the new students meeting.
Agnes: Hi! Welcome to O-Week! What's your subject?
Fouad: Chemistry. I'm in the science department.
Agnes: You're the first student to arrive at the meeting! I'm your student host. My name's Agnes. What's your name?
Fouad: Fouad. I'm from Saudi Arabia. I'm Saudi. Nice to meet you, Agnes!
Agnes: Nice to meet you too, Fouad!
Fouad: Are you from Australia?
Agnes: Not, I'm not. I'm a student here in Melbourne but I'm from Germany – I'm German.
Fouad: Oh. Where are you from in Germany?
Agnes: Berlin.
Fouad: Berlin? Is Berlin the capital of Germany?
Agnes: Yes, it is. Oh, excuse me. Here's another new student. Fouad, this is Yibo. Yibo, this is Fouad. Yibo's a science student too.
Fouad: Hi, Yibo. Nice to meet you.
Yibo: Hello, Fouad. Nice to meet you too.
Fouad: Where are you from, Yibo?
Yibo: I'm from China. I'm from Beijing.
Fouad: Really? My brother is a student in Beijing. He thinks Chinese food is very good!
Yibo: Yes, it is. It's very nice.
Agnes: Australian food is very good too. There's a free Barbie at the student union carnival on Friday.
Fouad / Yibo: 'Barbie'?
Agnes: Oh! I'm sorry! 'Barbie' is an informal word for 'barbeque' in Australia. We cook meat, or fish, or vegetables outside over a fire.
Fouad: I'd like to go. What about you, Yibo?
Yibo: Yes, please!
Agnes: OK, that's great. Now, let's just wait for a few more students to arrive and then we can start our tour of the campus!

Track 1.3
Fouad, this is Yibo. Yibo, this is Fouad. Yibo's a science student too.
Hi, Yibo. Nice to meet you.
Hello, Fouad. Nice to meet you too.

Track 1.4
/ɒ/ what /ei/ name /ai/ I

Track 1.5
from nice make day on my not they fine

Track 1.6
Hassan: Excuse me, are you Etsuko?
Etsuko: Yes, I am.
Hassan: Remember me? At the tour of the university – on Wednesday?
Etsuko: Oh yes! Of course! You're Ahmed!
Hassan: No, I'm not. My name's Hassan.
Etsuko: I'm sorry, Hassan. I remember now. You're from Turkey.
Hassan: No, I'm not. I'm from Iran. And you're from Japan!
Etsuko: That's right! You've got a good memory, Hassan! How are you?
Hassan: Fine, thanks. And you?
Etsuko: I'm OK too. There's a lot to do – O-Week is such a busy time!
Hassan: Yes, it is and I'm looking for a place to live too!
Etsuko: Oh really? Where are you at the moment?
Hassan: I'm in a room in a shared flat. It's right in the city centre and I can walk to the university in ten minutes. There are three of us in the flat.
Etsuko: How many rooms are there?
Hassan: Three.
Etsuko: Is your room big?
Hassan: No, it isn't. It's very small. But the other students are very friendly so I can practise my English! But it's very noisy. There isn't a quiet place for me to study.
Etsuko: Is there a desk?
Hassan: No, there isn't but there's a small table for my laptop. I go to the university library when I want to study. And there aren't any bookshelves so all my books are under the sofa. It's not ideal! What about you, Estuko? Where are you?
Etsuko: I'm in a room in a student hall. It's a single room. It's a bit small but there's everything I need. There's a big desk for my laptop, there's a lamp and there are bookshelves so there's lots of space for all my books. I love reading! There's a small sofa too – it's very comfortable! The best thing is that it's very quiet – and I can see the park from my window!
Hassan: I want to find a room like yours!

Track 1.7
My ideal room to study in? It's my bedroom at home. It's a big room and it's blue. Blue is a very calm colour. There's a big window, so it's very bright. There are three bookshelves, there's a large desk for my laptop and there's a red sofa. It's a good room to study in because it's very quiet and it's very tidy!

UNIT 2

Track 1.8
Etsuko: Hi Ahmed! How are you?
Ahmed: OK, but I'm freezing. It's minus 10 degrees today!
Etsuko: Yes, I know it's very cold, Ahmed. But, it IS January and Canada is the coldest country in the world!
Ahmed: I really don't like winter. It's awful.
Etsuko: No, it isn't! It's fantastic! I love it. The winter carnival starts this weekend – on Saturday! Do you want to come with me?
Ahmed: I'm not sure. What happens at the carnival?
Etsuko: Well, there are amazing snow sculptures all over the city and there is even an ice palace! It's very beautiful –

especially at night when the lights shine through the walls of ice. I really want to see it!

Ahmed: Well I don't! What's interesting about an ice palace? It's boring.

Etsuko: OK but you like sport – there's a canoe race across the St Lawrence River. It's one of the main attractions – it's very exciting!

Ahmed: I like playing sport – I don't like watching it. And I hate watching sport in the cold!

Etsuko: So you don't want to see the snow bathers then …

Ahmed: Snow bathers? Do you mean people actually have a bath in the snow!

Etsuko: Yes, can you imagine? Isn't that awful?

Ahmed: I feel freezing cold just thinking about it.

Etsuko: OK, Ahmed, do you want to come to the winter carnival or not? All you need are warm clothes!

Ahmed: I've got a coat and a scarf but I don't have a hat …

Etsuko: I've got a red one you can have. Come on, Ahmed! I really want you to meet Bonhomme!

Ahmed: Who's he?

Etsuko: He's a snowman! And he wears a bright red hat too!

Track 1.9

I really don't like winter. I like playing sport.
I love it. I hate watching sport in the cold!

Track 1.10

awful interesting fantastic exciting beautiful boring amazing colourful freezing delicious

Track 1.11

Fouad: Hi, Jing! Do you want to go to the *Festival of the Winds* next weekend?

Jing: The *Festival of the Winds?* What is that exactly?

Fouad: It's a kite festival! Look at the poster! It's a festival for people who love kites. It's only once a year, and lasts for one day. I don't want to miss it!

Jing: I'm not sure. I haven't got a kite.

Fouad: You don't need one! Kite fliers from all over Australia and all over the world come to show their kites and fly them. It's free, too.

Jing: So we don't pay? That sounds good! When is it?

Fouad: Next Sunday – Sunday the ninth.

Jing: I like the kites in the poster – lots of different shapes and sizes.

Fouad: They're amazing. There are even kites of huge cartoon characters and there are even flying trains and flying buildings!

Jing: So, is the festival just about kites?

Fouad: No it isn't. There is an entertainment programme too, with an art exhibition and different workshops too.

Jing: Is there a dance workshop?

Fouad: Yes, there is.

Jing: Fantastic! I love dancing.

Fouad: I don't! I'm a really bad dancer. But there is a kite-making workshop and I really want to go to that. I want to make my own kite and then fly it on the beach! There are also stalls with food and drink from around the world.

Jing: Mmm! Delicious!

Fouad: Do you want to come with me to the food stalls?

Jing: Yes, of course I do! You know I love food!

Fouad: How do we get to Bondi beach? I don't want to go by car – it's difficult to park close to the beach.

Jing: That's true. We can take a train to Bondi Junction and then catch a bus.

Fouad: Do you want to check the website and find out? The festival starts at 11am – we don't want to be late.

Jing: Good idea!

Track 1.12

Leah: An important day for me? Oh, that's easy! Singapore National Day is really special. It's on the 9th of August. What happens? Well, I spend the day with my family and friends. We watch the National Day parade on a live webcast! It's very colourful! Then we eat delicious chicken rice. I like it very much! I wear national costume too – we call it *Peranakan* dress – it's very beautiful! Why is the day special? Well, it's not just a public holiday to me – it's a day when I can celebrate everything about Singapore and be happy!

UNIT 3

Track 1.13

Katrin: Excuse me, Li Bo? Are you busy?

Li Bo: Not really. I'm trying to write an essay.

Katrin: I'd like to ask you a few questions.

Li Bo: Sure, what about?

Katrin: We're doing some research into new first-year students. It's for Student services. We're asking how new students feel.

Li Bo: Well, that's interesting, but why are you doing it?

Katrin: We want to see if confident students do better in their first year. Then we can help students who are quiet or feel a bit shy.

Li Bo: OK. Let's start.

Katrin: OK, first question. What do you say when friends ask you to go somewhere with them?

Li Bo: Let me think. I like it when they ask me. I usually feel happy.

Katrin: Really? You always say yes?

Li Bo: Yes, I do.

Katrin: OK, next question. What do you do when someone starts a conversation with you? Do you feel happy to talk, do you try to finish the conversation quickly or do you often feel shy?

Li Bo: Hmm. I am often a bit shy and get nervous when someone new talks to me, I think.

Katrin: OK. Let's go to the next question. Where do you usually like working or studying?

Li Bo: Uh, well, I don't like big groups or classes – I sometimes feel a bit shy in them. I don't really like talking in front of a lot of people. I like working at my desk.

Katrin: OK. Now, the next question is … how do other people describe you? What do they say about you?

Li Bo: Ooh – that's a difficult one. Well, they don't think I'm talkative, and they don't think I'm quiet.

Katrin: So they say you're warm and friendly?

Li Bo: Yes, I think so.

Katrin: Right, just one more question. What do you do when someone says something nice to you?

Li Bo: I like it when someone says something nice to me, like when my tutor says my essay is good – I always feel happy then.

Katrin: So, you feel good?

Li Bo: Yes.

Katrin: Thanks very much for your help, Li Bo.

Li Bo: No problem.

Audioscripts

Track 1.14

Grant: Thank you for coming today, Pilar.
Pilar: My pleasure.
Grant: Well, let's start. So the job is with Student Services – we're part of the university that tries to help the students with any problems.
Pilar: Yes, I looked at Student Services on the Internet.
Grant: Oh, really – good. Now, you have an MBA …
Pilar: Yes, from the University of Santiago. I really enjoyed doing it.
Grant: Yes, Spain is a wonderful country.
Pilar: Chile.
Grant: Sorry?
Pilar: Chile – Santiago is in Chile.
Grant: Ah, yes of course. So, do you like learning new things?
Pilar: Yes, I do.
Grant: Do you think you can learn on the job too?
Pilar: You mean, can I learn things when I'm working on them?
Grant: Yes – there's a lot to learn in this job. We're looking for someone who can learn quickly.
Pilar: I can do that.
Grant: Great. And you can speak three languages?
Pilar: Yes, I can speak English and Spanish, of course and my German is quite good too.
Grant: Why are you interested in the job?
Pilar: Well, I'm interested because I can work with international students. I lived abroad for one year so I know what it's like to study and work in another country. I know what problems international students can have.
Grant: Like understanding the Scottish accent.
Pilar: Yes, and understanding Scottish weather. So, I can help other international students because I understand their difficulties.
Grant: Great. And what about working in teams?
Pilar: I'm very good at teamwork. I help the other team members and I can communicate very well with other people.
Grant: Can you work well under pressure?
Pilar: Yes, I can. I always finish my work on time and I often work at weekends and evenings.
Grant: So you're very hardworking then?
Pilar: Yes, I am.
Grant: Do you have experience leading a team?
Pilar: No, I don't. But I do have experience leading projects.
Grant: So, do you feel that you can manage a team?
Pilar: Yes, I'm sure I can manage a team well. I have all the skills to do it and I'm sure I can do a good job.
Grant: OK, well let's talk more about your project management …

Track 1.15

1 I can manage a team.
2 Harold can't get a job.
3 Can you speak French?
4 Yes, I can.
5 Pilar can help too.
6 Can you take an IELTS test?

Track 1.16

A: Can you work well under pressure?
B: Yes, I can do that.
A: I can speak English and Spanish.
B: Yes, I can, too.

Track 1.17

Can you speak English?   Can you finish work on time?
Can you lead a team?   Can you work well under pressure?
Can you manage people? Can you listen to people?

Track 1.18

I'm very good at teamwork.
I'm quite good at teamwork.
I'm not bad at working under pressure.
I'm OK at working under pressure.
I can work well alone.
I can't work well in large groups.

Track 1.19

Examiner: OK, now can you tell me about a famous person you admire?
Drew: I really admire Leonardo DiCaprio. He's an actor, and he makes really good films. He's hardworking and funny – he makes me laugh. I really admire him because he is generous – he's rich and he uses his money to help people. He's also intelligent; he has a website about the environment and he wants to change the world.

Track 1.20

Examiner: So, can you talk about a famous person you admire?
Kavitha: I admire Bill Gates. He's a businessman from America. He is the leader of Microsoft and he's very rich. He's intelligent – he wrote a computer programme which changed the world. But I admire him because he's very kind and generous – he gives money to help people in poor countries.

UNIT 4

Track 1.21

geology   literature   languages   sociology   psychology   biology

Track 1.22

Dr Sawyer: Good afternoon, everyone. Today Esra is talking about changes in education. Are you ready?
Esra: Yes, I think so.
Dr Sawyer: OK, Esra, let's start.
Esra: A big change in education in my country is that more women are going to university and colleges. This is happening in many countries. Today I'm talking about the UK …
Dr Sawyer: Not your country?
Esra: No, Dr Sawyer – I'm taking another country as an example.
Dr Sawyer: I see.
Esra: So, some years ago in Britain the number of women in higher education went up until there were more women than men. Today 49.2 per cent of women are now studying at university, with only 37.2 per cent of men at university. There is a 12% difference in the number of men and women at university in the UK. Two other things are important: the kind of qualification women get and the subjects they choose. The percentage of men getting a good degree at university is nearly 60%. But almost 64% of women at university are getting good degrees. Another important thing is that more men leave university early than

women. Women students are successfully finishing their courses.

Dr Sawyer: So what about the type of course? Is it still true that more men take science subjects than women?

Esra: Well, research shows that there are more women on most courses, especially in law and medicine. But in maths, computer science and engineering there are more men than women. In computer science just under 20% of students are women and 80% are men. In engineering just 14% of students are women and 86% are men. So more men than women are taking science subjects.

John: And is this just in Britain?

Esra: No, this is the same in many other countries and in Arab countries too. So one of the main changes in education is the rising number of women and the fact that women are doing well – this is something we can be proud of.

Track 1.23

1 39.9   **2** 80.1   **3** 12%

Track 1.24

39   39.9   18.1   80.1   12%   2%

Track 1.25

Examiner: Can you tell me what you're studying at the moment, Adel?

Adel: At the moment I am an undergraduate student. I'm studying biology at King Saud University in Riyadh in Saudi Arabia. It's a good place to learn and I'm really enjoying my course. Biology is about living things. I'm interested in biology because I want to understand how life started.

Examiner: Yun, tell me about your education.

Yun: I'm studying at the University of Wuhan in China. My subject is sociology – that's the study of society. It's a master's degree so it's quite difficult. I'm interested in it because society is changing very quickly in China. I want to understand how these changes affect us.

Examiner: Esra, can you tell me about what you're studying?

Esra: I'm from Oman, but I'm studying in Scotland at the University of Glasgow. It's a great place to study. I'm taking a masters in psychology – educational psychology. Educational psychology is the study of how people learn in education. I want to find out why there are more women in education. I find it fascinating.

Track 1.26

It's a good place to learn.	My subject is sociology.
It's a great place to study.	I'm interested in biology.
I'm studying biology.	I find it fascinating.

UNIT 5

Track 1.27

Tao: Sorry, can you help me?

Karen: Sure.

Tao: I'm trying to find the Business School.

Karen: Oh, yes, the Business School. That's easy. You see that big, old building?

Tao: Yes, it's amazing.

Karen: That's the Gilbert Scott building. The Business School is in there.

Tao: Thanks.

Ann: Excuse me, I'm looking for the restaurant. Can you tell me where it is?

Nikki: Sure, it's opposite the library. Can you see the modern building made of glass and stone?

Ann: I think so. The one with green and blue glass?

Nikki: Yes, that's it. That's the Fraser building – you can get sandwiches and hot food there.

Pilar: Excuse me. Can you help me? I'm looking for the library.

Lee: The main library?

Pilar: Yes.

Lee: OK. Look over there at that huge, tall, concrete building. That's the library. It's next to the art gallery.

Pilar: Yes, I can see it.

Lee: The information desk is at the front door.

Pilar: Thanks.

Track 1.28

Alan: Good evening and welcome to Great Designs, where we look at some amazing buildings. I'm Alan Davies, and tonight I'm talking to Professor Gu Ying about a building that wasn't here for a long time. In fact it was only here for six months but the ideas for the building are still with us today. Professor Gu Ying works in London, and knows all about the building of the Seed Cathedral – which many people visited in the Shanghai Expo. Professor Gu, welcome to the programme … How did the project start?

Gu: Well, the seed bank in London was the starting point. We collected seeds from all over the world for the future. Then, in 2010 Thomas Heatherwick decided to use the seeds for the UK building in the Shanghai World Fair in China.

Alan: It was an amazing building.

Gu: Yes, it was. It was fantastic. There were thousands of clear plastic rods which were very flexible and moved in the wind. These rods weren't very big – in fact, they were very small – and there were seeds at the end of each rod. So, in the daytime, there was a lot of natural light in the building because sunlight came inside through the rods. And at night the rods lit up, as there was a small light inside each one.

Alan: How many rods were there?

Gu: I think there were about 60 000.

Alan: Was there any special reason for the design?

Gu: Well, Heatherwick didn't want a lot of high technology in his building. He wanted to show the main idea of the Shanghai World Fair. This was 'Better City, Better Life'.

Alan: Better City, Better Life? A very simple idea!

Gu: Yes, it was. He liked all the beautiful parks and gardens in the city of London, and he wanted to show that nature can make a city a better place to live in.

Alan: Were you at the building when it was in Shanghai?

Gu: Yes, I was. I was there many times.

Alan: Was it very special?

Gu: Yes, it was. It was very peaceful and quiet inside the cathedral. It was very popular – people loved the idea.

Alan: What happened to all the seeds after the World Fair closed?

Gu: Well, that's one of the best things about the whole project. After the fair, all the rods were presented to schools in China and the UK to keep. It really was a very great success.

Alan: That's very good to know. Thank you very much for talking to me about it, Professor Gu.

Gu: Thank you, Alan.

Audioscripts

Track 1.29

1 started   2 designed   3 liked

Track 1.30

liked   started   designed   completed   used   believed called   celebrated   finished

Track 1.31

Kinga: A special building? Well, Sydney Opera House is very special for me. It's in Sydney, of course, in the east of Australia. What do I know about it? Well, it's a really spectacular building. The designer was from Denmark. I think his name was Jorn Utzon. He changed his plans for the building many times and the construction work took a long time – fifteen years I think! Why is it special for me? I love the shape of the roof. It's completely unique. It's amazing in daylight and it looks very dramatic at night too. People from all over the world see it as a landmark of Australia. It represents my country and I'm very proud of it.

Track 1.32

It's a really spectacular building …
It's amazing in daylight …
It looks very dramatic at night …
It's definitely my favourite building …

UNIT 6

Track 1.33

Sebastien: Hi Monika! You look busy – what are you doing?
Monika: I AM busy! I want to help as a volunteer in the student welcome centre and I need to apply online.
Sebastien: Ah yes! I saw an advertisement in the student union. I'm not surprised they need helpers for the student welcome centre! It's always so busy there. It was really busy when we first arrived as new students. I can't believe that was two years ago!
Monika: I know – it's amazing! I met you in the queue on the very first day of the semester!
Sebastien: That's right! In fact, we waited so long that we got to know each other really well!
Monika: Yes, we spent an hour in that queue and you told me about your family in Switzerland …
Sebastien: And you felt very excited about starting your new life here.
Monika: I remember! We talked so much that by the time we got to the front of the queue we didn't remember what we wanted to ask!
Sebastien: That's right! I can't believe that we came here two years ago!
Monika: I know – it's amazing.
Sebastien: So do you really want to be a volunteer?
Monika: Yes, I do.
Sebastien: But you don't have any work experience.
Monika: That's true, but I've got experience of being a student. I understand how new students feel when they leave their own country and arrive in a completely new place. I really missed my family and friends when I left Brazil. I had so many questions so it was good to talk to the volunteers.
Sebastien: That's true. I found them really easy to talk to and they gave me some really useful advice too. But you don't get paid to be a volunteer.
Monika: I don't care about that. I just want to do something

different and help people at the same time. Why don't you apply to become a volunteer too? What do you say?
Sebastien: I'm not sure. I'll think about it …

Track 1.34

Jakub: Hi Hiromi! How was your holiday?
Hiromi: Hi Jakub! It was great. I didn't go back to Japan though. I didn't have enough money for that so I stayed here. Actually, I spent most of the time working!
Jakub: You worked all holiday? I didn't know. What did you do?
Hiromi: I was a sandwich artist.
Jakub: A sandwich artist! What's that? It sounds very important.
Hiromi: I made sandwiches in a cafe!
Jakub: Oh! I'd like to do that. Chicken Caesar is my favourite! Did you eat the sandwiches too?
Hiromi: No I didn't! I made so many sandwiches the last thing I wanted to do was eat them! I always had salad for lunch. I didn't just make sandwiches though, I served customers too. I felt very nervous about that at first because I didn't feel confident about my English. But most of the people who came into the shop were really friendly. In fact, I began to really enjoy talking to them. Talking to people became the best part of the job for me! It made me happy. It was a really early start though. I got up at 6am every morning and began work at 7am.
Jakub: You got up at 6am!
Hiromi: Yes! I didn't like that – in fact, one morning I slept really late and didn't get to work until 8!
Jakub: So, how many hours did you work?
Hiromi: 6 hours a day so – 30 hours a week.
Jakub: 30 hours? I thought that students couldn't work more than 20 hours.
Hiromi: We can't work more than 20 hours during semester. But you can work as many hours as you want during the holidays. I went to the student centre to check that before I took the job.
Jakub: So did you work Monday to Friday?
Hiromi: Yes, weekdays only so I had time to relax on Saturdays and Sundays. In fact, I spent most of my weekends on the beach!
Jakub: I think I need to find a job too.
Hiromi: That's a good idea. I found it a really useful experience. I feel much more confident about my English now and I made some money too! So next mid holiday I can go back to Japan!
Jakub: Do you think I could be a sandwich artist too?
Hiromi: Of course you could. After all, you love food!
Jakub: So, can you give me the address of the sandwich shop you worked in?
Hiromi: Yes, of course I can. Now, where did I put my pen …?

Track 1.35

I felt very nervous.   I didn't feel confident.
It made me happy.

Track 1.36

Jing: Last summer I worked as a school holiday assistant. What did I do? Well, I had to think of different activities and games to play with the kids in the morning and in the afternoons we took them on trips to museums or the zoo. I'm really glad I did it – it was really challenging because I had to think about different ways to keep the children happy and busy! I had to be quite flexible too. Kids can get bored very quickly, you know! The best thing was that it was relevant to my psychology course. I'm so glad I did it!

Agnes: A time when I did something rewarding? Well, I really enjoyed it when I spent a few weeks picking fruit in Tasmania. We began work early in the morning and didn't finish until early evening. Well, it wasn't exactly hard work but it was quite tiring. Why was it so rewarding? Well, the money was good but I also liked the social life. I made some good friends with students from all over the world. In fact, I met my boyfriend there too, so that was an added benefit!

Track 1.37

1 help
2 answer
3 sleep

Track 1.38

speaker	well paid	welcome
picture	read	confident
friendly	week	meet

UNIT 7

Track 1.39

a No, I don't have to. I finished it yesterday.
b Yes, I have to start at 7.30.
c No, I don't have to, but I want to see the Manager.
d I have to come to class everyday.

Track 1.40

Dee Dee: Hello.
Bob: Hi, Dee Dee – Bob here, Joey and I need some help.
Dee Dee: Sure, go ahead.
Bob: I'm on North Main Street with Joey. We've got a clue from *City Hunt*. Can you help us?
Dee Dee: What is it?
Bob: OK. It says: 'Your next challenge is in Japan. Can you find the place where man went into space?'
Dee Dee: Space. Challenge. Japan? … It's got to be the Challenger Space Shuttle Memorial statue.
Bob: Great. But in Japan?
Dee Dee: It's in Little Tokyo.
Bob: Great – Joey, there's a taxi, stop it!
Dee Dee: No, Bob . You can't go by taxi. You have to walk. Go south to East 1st Street and walk for two blocks. It's at the Weller Court building.
….
Joey: Hey, Dee Dee. We found the Space Shuttle Memorial.
Dee Dee: Yes, I can see you on the Internet. You have to take a photo and send it to me. I can put it on the website.
Joey: OK – I'm sending it now.
Dee Dee: Send me the next clue too.
Joey: Right.
Dee Dee: Got it. A mouse and the Lion King come here to play and sing.
Joey: That's really difficult.
Dee Dee: Well, the Lion King is an old cartoon.
Joey: And the mouse is Mickey Mouse …
Dee Dee: Got it! It's the Walt Disney Concert Hall.
Joey: That's South Grand Avenue. That's near you.
Dee Dee: Yeah, but I can't go there, it's not allowed. You

have to go there, and quickly. I can see the next team is very close to you.
Joey: How do we get there?
Dee Dee: Go back to 1st Street. Then take a bus back to Grand Avenue. Hurry!

Track 1.41

Sofia: Hello, everyone. Now, how many people came here by car? That's quite a lot. Think about this – over 70% of car journeys are less than five kilometres. As you know, it's the start of fitness week, so why don't you change your daily routine a little and become healthy too? Let's look at some really easy ways to exercise. These are all activities that don't need special equipment and don't cost a lot of money.

First, walking. We are walking less and less – 20% less than thirty years ago. But walking helps your heart and lungs and improves the strength in your muscles and bones. If you don't do a lot of activity at the moment, you can try walking to the shop instead of going by car, or getting off the bus one stop before your work and walking the extra distance. After a bit of practice, you can try power-walking. Power-walking is walking very fast – almost running.

When your fitness improves, you can try jogging. Jogging is a great way to keep fit – just take it easy at the start. Try to increase your jogging time by 10% each week until you're jogging for 30 minutes three times a week. Like walking, jogging is good for your heart and lungs, your bones and muscles. You can give yourself targets. One day say that you are jogging to the end of the street. On the next day, say you're jogging to the end of the next street. Find a jogging partner and make a plan together.

Swimming is also a good way to exercise. Although swimming doesn't make your bones strong, it is good for your heart, lungs and your muscles. You can swim as fast or as slow as you like, but the important thing is to keep going. Swimming for long periods is good for burning calories and reducing fat. Again, you can find a partner to swim with or join a club.

Cycling is an excellent way to exercise – just 30 minutes of cycling burns 300 calories. Like swimming, cycling doesn't help to keep your bones strong. But like walking and jogging, cycling can be part of your daily life. For people who travel a short distance to work, cycling can be very good for you. Like swimming, cycling doesn't help to keep our bones strong, but it is very good for our heart and lungs.

So you see we can all make small changes in our lives to help us stay healthy. Now, who wants to sign the Keeping Fit Form?

Track 1.42

Examiner: OK, Valeria, can you talk about the task card?
Valeria: I like such a lot of sports, but my favourite sport is volleyball. It's absolutely great! You can play it in so many places: inside on a court, or outside in a park. You can even play it on the beach! The rules are really easy. You play in teams of six people. You have to hit a ball over the net. You score a point by hitting the ball onto the ground on the other team's side of the net. You have to use your hands to hit the ball, you can't use your head or feet. It's really easy to learn – anyone can play it. It's my favourite sport because it's very fast and exciting. I really like to get together with friends and play volleyball on the beach. It's such a lot of fun.

Track 1.43

You can **even** play it on the beach.	It's **absolutely** great!
You can play it in **so** many places.	It's **very** fast.
I like **such** a lot of sports.	It's **really** easy to learn.

Audioscripts

UNIT 8

Track 2.1

Erik: Hi Leah! Have you got plans for the holidays?

Leah: Yeah, I have. I'm going to Australia!

Erik: Australia? Wow! That sounds great.

Leah: I know! I'm so excited! I've been online and read quite a lot about it. And I've seen some fantastic photos too – the scenery is very beautiful all along the coastline. Have you ever been to Australia, Erik?

Erik: Yes, I have! I've only been to the south-east, but it was amazing.

Leah: When was that?

Erik: I was there last summer with a few friends. Have you heard of the Great Ocean Road? It's is a very long road that goes along the coast.

Leah: Yes, I know! I've read that it's 234 kilometres long!

Erik: That's right. Well, we drove along part of the road, as far as Great Otway National Park. It has really thick rainforests. The trees were so close together it was difficult to see where we were going! In fact, we nearly got lost! We saw some spectacular views, too.

Leah: I've read that there are lots of sandy beaches all along the coastline – I really want to spend some of my holiday relaxing by the sea. I always do that on holiday, and always have! Did you spend any time on the beach?

Erik: Yes, we did, but it wasn't exactly relaxing! I went surfing. The waves were amazing – I've never seen waves like them. It was really exciting.

Leah: Surfing! That's exciting. I've never tried surfing. I don't know if I could keep my balance!

Erik: You never know till you've tried! It only took me a few days to learn how to stand on the board!

Leah: Em … I'm not sure. I'd rather stay on dry land and enjoy some wildlife at Tower Hill. Have you heard of Tower Hill?

Erik: No, I haven't.

Leah: Tower Hill's an extinct volcano. You can see all kinds of birds and animals there. I've read it's a great place to see kangaroos and koalas. I've seen them in the zoo of course – when I was about five years old! I've never seen them in the wild before.

Erik: I'm the same. I've only seen them in the zoo. I'd love to see them in their natural habitat.

Leah: Me too. Have you got any plans for the summer?

Erik: No.

Leah: Great! I've just had a brilliant idea …

Track 2.2

Australia? Wow! That sounds great.

Surfing! That's exciting.

Track 2.3

1 Have you ever been to Australia?
3 Has she ever seen a kangaroo?

2 Yes, I have.
4 No, she hasn't.

Track 2.4

Sergei: Hi, Caz! I haven't seen you for ages! Where have you been?

Caz: Hi Sergei! I've been in Costa Rica for the last four weeks!

Sergei: Costa Rica? Wow! I've never been to Central America!

Caz: It was an amazing experience. I worked on a conservation project.

Sergei: Conservation project? What do you mean exactly?

Caz: Well, I have been interested in animals since I was a child and I've always loved turtles. They are my favourite animals! So, I decided to work as a volunteer on a sea turtle project – to protect sea turtles and their nests on the beach.

Sergei: So, what did you do exactly?

Caz: Well, I spent a lot of time checking the nests. I counted the baby turtles – that was definitely the best part! I also helped to clean up the beach and we even went on night patrols of the beach – there was a lot to do but it was very rewarding.

Sergei: So, did you have any free time?

Caz: Oh yes! It wasn't all about work! One day I went rafting!

Sergei: Rafting? You mean you only had a platform of wood to protect you from the water! I've never done that! It sounds very dangerous!

Caz: No, it wasn't – it was exciting! It was a great experience to go down the river so fast. I'm so glad that I did it! We also went walking around the base of Arenal Volcano.

Sergei: I've never seen a volcano! Is it extinct?

Caz: Well, not exactly but it's not active very often. We had a spectacular view – I took lots of photographs! And another time we went to the rainforest. I've never seen so many different colours in one place – the butterflies were so beautiful and I loved the waterfalls. I'd definitely like to go back one day. It's the best trip I've ever had!

Track 2.5

Hiromi: A special place of natural beauty? Well, Mount Fuji is very special for me. It is in the south-west of Japan. It's the highest mountain in our country – it's nearly four thousand metres high. It's spectacular so many artists have painted it! I've been to Mount Fuji. I went a long time ago – I think I was six years old. I can still remember it – we went in July. What is special about it for me? That's easy! It's always changing! When we saw it it was light purple in colour but I've also seen photographs where it is snowy and grey! The way it changes colour makes it very special for me. It's also special because it's a symbol of my country – of Japan.

UNIT 9

Track 2.6

Fouad: Hi Jing! What are you doing?

Jing: I'm looking at some photos. Do you want to see them?

Fouad: I'd love to! Hey! Is that a red egg? I've never seen an egg that colour before!

Jing: It's a present from my brother Lee. Look. That's him in that photo. He's older than me. He's twenty six. And that's his wife Yibo – she's my sister-in-law. They met before Lee did his military service and they got married when he came back! Yibo is an engineer. We really get on well together. She's like a sister to me.

Fouad: Who's that cute baby? She's adorable.

Jing: That's Zu. He's a baby boy, actually! He's Lee and Yibo's son. So now I'm an aunt. Zu's really funny – he's always smiling.

Fouad: So, that means Zu is your nephew?

Jing: That's right. I'm Zu's aunt and Zu is my nephew! This photo was taken at his Red Egg and Ginger party last weekend.

Fouad: Red Egg and Ginger party?

Jing: Yes, when people have a child, they celebrate a baby's first month birthday with a big party for family and friends. It's a really important event for us. People often have this party in a restaurant but we had our party for Zu at my parents' home in Beijing. Look – there's my father there and there's my mother. They're very proud of their new grandson. My mum's amazing. She's just got her driving licence at the age of 62!

Fouad: Well, you're never too old to learn!

Jing: That's true! All the guests get presents from the baby's parents when they arrive at the party. Eggs are symbols of change and they are coloured red because in China red means happiness!

Fouad: So, that's why you've got a red egg. What about the babies? Are they given presents too?

Jing: Oh, yes! They get red envelopes with money inside! But they're given other gifts too. Look at Zu's hat! Do you see the little tiger on it? In China the tiger is a very important animal – the king of all animals. It is believed that the tiger looks after babies and protects them from harm. That's why babies often get presents of tiger hats or tiger shoes. The tiger shoes usually have little eyes on them to guide the baby when they first learn to walk.

Fouad: Who's that old woman standing behind you in the photo? She looks very happy!

Jing: Oh! That's my grandmother and her husband's standing next to her – he's my grandfather. They got married just after they left school! They're very happy together.

Fouad: She's holding a pair of shoes too.

Jing: So she is. And what a surprise! There's a tiger at the front of each one!

Fouad: Looks like your nephew's got two tigers looking after him!

Track 2.7

Jakub: What an amazing photograph. You look so different in these clothes!

Hiromi: Yes, I look very formal! It's my coming of age ceremony. It's celebrated by all young people of the age of twenty.

Jakub: Twenty?

Hiromi: Yes, twenty is the age we become adults. It's called the age of majority in Japan. Twenty is the age when we get the vote. The ceremony is held every year in January. It's always held on a Monday and it's always the second Monday in January. This day is a national holiday in Japan.

Jakub: Do you all wear special clothes?

Hiromi: Girls wear special kimonos. The kimono I'm wearing is the same kimono my mum wore when she was twenty! I'm wearing her white scarf and the same sandals on my feet too! Boys can wear *hakama*, which is the male version of a kimono but they usually wear Western business suits.

Jakub: Your kimono is so beautiful. I really like the sleeves!

Hiromi: They're really long – about one metre long! That's why they are called 'swinging sleeves'. It's the most formal kimono for single women. Older married women wear short-sleeved kimonos.

Jakub: What about the belt? It's very beautiful.

Hiromi: Yes, that's an *obi*. It's a very wide belt which is worn around the waist. It's the most expensive part of the kimono. It's so expensive, in fact, that many families have to hire them.

Jakub: So what happens during the ceremony?

Hiromi: Well, the ceremony varies from place to place. Some have performances and speeches, others only have speeches. We listen to government officials talking about what it means to be an adult and the importance of being responsible. We are also given money. It's an important part of the day.

Jakub: What happens after the ceremony?

Hiromi: Most people go to parties or bars to celebrate with friends. We eat red bean rice. This is always eaten when there's something to celebrate! Well, you are only twenty once!

Jakub: That's true!

Track 2.8

Ana: An important life event in my country? Well, I do think that getting a driving licence is a very important life event in Brazil for young people. You can't learn until you're 18. This is the age we become adults – we're no longer children! How do we prepare? Well, it's far from easy. It really does takes a very long time. In fact, I really do think it can be compared to a very long journey! This is because we have to pass several tests. I think there are four altogether – psychological, theoretical, technical and practical. Why is it important? Well, it's important to get your driving licence because it's needed for many jobs in Brazil. What I like most is the independence it brings – the freedom to get in my car and drive where I want. It's a truly fantastic feeling!

Track 2.9

I **do** think that getting a driving licence is a very important life event in Brazil.

It's **far** from easy.

It **really does** take a very long time.

I **really do** think that it can be compared to a very long journey.

What I like most is the independence it brings.

It's a **truly** fantastic feeling!

UNIT 10

Track 2.10

Esra: OK, so the next thing we're talking about is Earth Day – the day of conservation groups.

Alex: Yes, we're all in the Ecology Society. Let's organise something this year.

Esra: That's right, Alex – we didn't do anything last year.

Carol: We could put up some posters.

Esra: Or hand out some leaflets.

Alex: Yes, we could give out some leaflets about Earth Day.

Carol: That's OK, but what happens then? We put up posters and give out our leaflets and then what?

Alex: I see what you mean. Giving out information isn't really celebrating Earth Day. Let's look at some ideas from Earth Day Network.

Carol: OK.

Esra: Here's one – planting trees – how about that?

Alex: It's not a bad idea, but how much time have we got? There are only two months before Earth Day.

Esra: We could ask students to buy a tree and plant it on campus for Earth Day.

Carol: Esra, you can't just plant trees around the University. Look at this one – this looks good. What about a concert?

Alex: Yeah – we can get two or three bands.

Esra: I can find a speaker to talk about Earth Day.

Alex: We can hold it at the Student Theatre.

Carol: It sounds like a good idea, but it could be difficult to organise.

Esra: What do you mean?

Carol: Think about bringing the band to the theatre and selling drinks. Have we really got enough time to do this? And there's some money for the Ecology Society, but do we have enough money?

Esra: Carol's right – it could be too difficult.

Audioscripts

Alex: Yes, it's a good idea, but we can't make a decision today. So Carol, what's your suggestion?
Carol: How about a campus clean up? It can't be too difficult to organise and it includes lots of people – staff and students. I'm sure we could get people to do it – we just meet everyone and say where they can collect litter.
Esra: And there are lots of places to clean up on campus.
Alex: You bet – we could start with my room!
Esra: Ugh, yuck.
Carol: No thanks, Alex.

Track 2.11

Professor Aldred: … and the next thing to talk about is the Red List. What is the Red List? Well, it is a list of animals in very serious danger. Animal extinction is part of nature, but humans are making this happen between a 100 and a 1 000 times faster than happens naturally.

There are many reasons for this. All of them are connected to human activity. Let's look at three threats to animals – pollution, hunting and climate change. The first part of my talk is about pollution. Some animals are affected badly by water pollution. Let's look at two examples. First, in South America, otters died when chemicals went into their rivers. Second, at sea, oil pollution causes illness in dolphins.

The earth is a big place, but humans are moving into areas where animals live. The problem is that animals need their environment. When we cut down forests we destroy the animals' habitats. Let's look at the mountain gorilla. These animals live in the mountain forests of Africa. But people have cut down their forest homes for farming and there are just under 800 of these beautiful animals in the world now.

So, animals are in danger from pollution and destruction of their environment. But others are hunted – we find and kill them to sell them. Let's take an example – the black rhino. Between the 1970s and 80s the number of black rhinos fell by 96% because of hunting. Luckily, people do not want to buy products made from the black rhino anymore.

But a much bigger problem is affecting the polar bear. The problem is climate change – the earth becoming warmer. Polar bears live in the Arctic, where effects of climate change can be easily seen. Polar bears hunt on the sea ice. But now the ice is melting earlier, which means that the bears have a shorter time to find food.

So, now let's look at ways of helping these animals …

Track 2.12

destruction   pollution   conservation   extinction

Track 2.13

Examiner: OK. Can you tell me what you think the biggest environmental problem is and the reasons for this.
Veena: I'm not sure, but I think the main problem is not recycling enough. I guess people always want to buy the latest things – new clothes, a new mobile phone or car. We use them for a short time, then we want the next new thing. I think recycling more can help. By recycling, we don't use up resources and we can use the old things again. I try to help by using things I don't need again. I give things to charity or sell them online, or when they really are not good, I recycle them.

Track 2.14

1 I think the main problem is not recycling enough.
2 I guess people always want to buy the latest things.
3 I'm not sure.

UNIT 11

Track 2.15

lighter   faster   cheaper   longer

Track 2.16

It's lighter than this one.
It's faster than the others.
It's much cheaper than before.
It lasts longer than the others.

Track 2.17

Professor Findlay: Hello everyone, welcome to today's talk on modern design. Today Susan Meyer, from German engineering company MET, is talking about design engineering. Susan …
Susan: Thanks, Professor Findlay. Today design engineers work in the top jobs at some of the world's biggest companies. Some of these include Apple's Jonathan Ive, Muji's Naoto Fukasawa, and Dyson's James Dyson. The first part of my talk is about what design engineering is and the skills design engineers need. In the second part, I'm talking about the ideas behind good design engineering.

So first of all what is a design engineer? A design engineer researches what things or products people like to buy. They also develop ideas for new products. They work in many different areas of industry from computers to vacuum cleaners. A design engineer manages the process of making something from idea to product. For this reason they work with lots of people. What skills does a design engineer need? Let's look at three things. First, they need to be good at engineering and they may have an education in art and design. Next, they are creative and can think of new ideas. Many engineering projects are answers to questions like *Can we make this product better?* Third, they are good at solving problems. Design engineers don't just think of ideas, they also think of ways to make their ideas real.

Let me give you some examples of this. James Dyson designed a new vacuum cleaner and made it more efficient. His company takes ordinary machines like hand driers or air fans and uses modern technology to make the product different and work better. In Japan, Naoto Fukasawa looked at CD players and made the design simpler. Fukasawa has also designed mobile phones and other products. He believes good design comes from nature and the environment.

Design engineers need a good understanding of engineering. But design engineers can't do everything. To make a product in the modern world we need a team of people. Design engineers need good teamwork skills and need to be good at communicating. Probably the most famous design engineer in the world is Apple's Jonathan Ive. He developed a new way of carrying music around with us in our pocket. Jonathan Ive always says that success is because of his team. He works with a small team in an open office space. All the team work with the same ideas – to keep Apple's products simple and easy to use.

So, we have three sides of the job: firstly, researching products and thinking of good ideas; secondly, working in a team to bring the product to manufacture. And the third thing? A good business mind: design engineers need a good knowledge of business. Design engineers know how to design products that people want to buy. And this is why they have moved into top jobs in business.

Now let's turn to the ideas behind good design engineering …

Track 2.18

Megumi: Oh, er. Let me think. Um, my favourite object that I bought recently is probably my new smartphone. I got it a few weeks ago – I bought it online, actually. I needed it because I lost my old one. I'm always losing things! This phone was good value. I'm a student and the most important thing for me is price. I like it a lot because it has the same features as the others but it's much cheaper.

Caroline: What's my favourite object that I bought recently? It's definitely a pair of shoes. I love them so much. I bought them in a designer store last week. I went to a party on Saturday, and I wanted something new to wear. They are bright red and they look really stylish and unusual. I've never seen anything like them.

Mohammed: I don't know! I haven't bought anything recently! Let me think … Well, I'm wearing my smart watch. I bought it in Singapore last summer. I got it because it's just so amazing. Look, when you press here it becomes a phone, press here and it plays music. Look, you can even watch videos. Isn't that cool? It's very well-designed and it's lighter than a mobile phone. I really like it.

Track 2.19

I like it a lot.   I love them so much.   I really like it.

UNIT 12

Track 2.20

Raoul: Hi there, Izabela! What are you doing?

Izabela: I'm doing research for my gap year.

Raoul: Gap year? Are you going to take a whole year out after university?

Izabela: Yes, I am! It's probably the only time in my life that I'll have that length of time to travel and see the world. And of course it will give me time to think about what I want to do in the future.

Raoul: I suppose it will give you time to think about your options. Where are thinking of going? Somewhere in Europe?

Izabela: Well I've travelled all over France, Germany and Russia so I feel I know Europe quite well.

Raoul: That's true. And didn't you spend last summer in Sweden and Denmark?

Izabela: Yes, I did and I really enjoyed it. But the world's a big place and I'd like to see some more of it! I want to go somewhere completely new and different. So, my plan is to spend a few months in Asia and then go on to Australia!

Raoul: Are you sure about that? What about the cost? It will be too expensive.

Izabela: It won't be too bad. And I'm not just going to travel. I'm going to earn some money during the year too. My plan is to look for temporary jobs to help pay my way. I'd love to do fruit picking in Australia!

Raoul: I'm still not sure. It sounds like a complete waste of time to me. And how will a gap year look to a future employer? It will look like you just want to have one long holiday!

Izabela: No, it won't. It will show an employer that I'm independent and can think for myself. And it also shows that I am confident enough to face different challenges. A gap year will make me stand out from other people in a good way. And, you know what they say, Raoul – travel broadens the mind!

Track 2.21

1 Are you going out this evening?
2 Is she going to do a gap year?

Track 2.22

1 I'm not going! I don't want to.
2 Are you going to take a whole year out of university?
3 Where are you thinking of going?
4 I can't believe she's not going.
5 They're going to go travelling next year.
6 I'll go if you're going.

Track 2.23

Lucia: I'm going to tell you about my plans for the future. I'm going to study software engineering at University in Umea, a small city in the North of Sweden. I'm going to start next year, in October. I'm extremely excited about it. It's going to be an amazing learning experience. I really can't wait! But I'm slightly nervous too! Why is it important to me? Well, it's rather hard to say. There are so many reasons. Well, let me see. First of all, it's a really good university, so I'm sure I'll learn a lot. But I'm also very interested in living in another country and learning a new language – that's Swedish of course! It's a wonderful opportunity to enjoy myself, make friends and study something I really like. I'm certainly going to make the most of the experience!

Grammar reference

UNIT 1 HOME
PRESENT SIMPLE OF *BE*

You use the verb *be* to give information about yourself, other people, things and places.
*I **am** from Russia.*
*Moscow **is** a very big city.*
*They **are** new students.*

	+	−
I	**am** German.	am not (**I'm not**) Saudi.
You / we / they	**are** new students.	are not (**aren't**) from Oman.
He / she / it	**is** a student in Beijing.	is not (**isn't**) a teacher.

Questions and short answers

	+	−
Are you / we / they from Australia?	Yes, I **am**. Yes, you **are**. Yes, we **are**. Yes, they **are**.	No, I'm **not**. No, you **aren't**. No, we **aren't**. No, they **aren't**.
Is Berlin the capital of Germany?	Yes, it **is**.	No, it **isn't**.
Is she in Melbourne?	Yes, she **is**.	No, she **isn't**.

1 Choose the correct answers.
- **a** We *is / are* from Italy.
- **b** I *am / is* a university student.
- **c** *Is / Are* she in our class?
- **d** They *am / are* from Germany.
- **e** *Is / Are* you from Syria? Yes, *I'm / I am*.

THERE IS / THERE ARE

You use *there is* with singular nouns and *there are* with plural nouns.
***There is** a desk. / **There isn't** a window.*
***There are** books. / **There aren't** bookshelves.*

	+	−
Singular	There **is** a bed.	There **isn't** a shopping mall.
Plural	There **are** four beds.	There **aren't** bookshelves.

Questions and short answers

	+	−
Is there a park?	Yes, there **is**.	No, there **isn't**.
Are there others?	Yes, there **are**.	No, there **aren't**.
Is she in Sydney?	Yes, she **is**.	No, she **isn't**.

2 Complete the sentences with the correct form of *there is / there are*.
- **a** 'Is there a sofa?' 'Yes, there is .'
- **b** '_____ bookshelves?' 'No, _____ .'
- **c** '_____ beds?' 'Yes, _____ four beds.'
- **d** '_____ a park near the house?' 'Yes, _____ two parks.'

UNIT 2 FESTIVALS
PRESENT SIMPLE

You use the present simple to talk about things which are always or generally true.
The national language of Saudi Arabia is Arabic.
You also use the present simple to talk about things you do regularly, including habits.
*I **live** in Shanghai.*
*I **play** tennis on Tuesdays.*

I You We They	**live** **don't live**	in Quebec.
He She It	**lives** **doesn't live**	

1 Complete the sentences with *don't* or *doesn't*.
- **a** Hans _____ speak English.
- **b** They _____ have a cold winter in Sydney.
- **c** I _____ like English food.
- **d** It _____ snow here every year.

There are spelling rules for *he / she / it*. Most verbs add -*s*, but others change.

	Verb	Rule
1	ends in a consonant + -*y*	change -*y* to -*ies*
2	ends in -*s*, -*ch* or -*sh*	add -*es*
3	*do* and *go*	add -*es*

2 Which spelling rule does each word fit? Write 1, 2 or 3.
- **a** misses 2
- **b** does ___
- **c** flies ___
- **d** finishes ___
- **e** goes ___
- **f** watches ___

PRESENT SIMPLE QUESTIONS

Use the auxiliary verb *do* or *does* to form questions in the present simple.

Do	I / you / we / they	**live** in Canada?
Does	he / she /it	

Question words come before the auxiliary.

What / When Where / Why What time How long How much	do does	people the parade the shows	do? start? take place? last? cost?

3 Rearrange the words to make questions.
- **a** speak / Spanish / your friend / does
- **b** you / here / come / often / do
- **c** does / start / the party / when
- **d** do / work / finish / what time / you

UNIT 3 TEAMWORK
ADVERBS OF FREQUENCY

You use adverbs of frequency to say how often you do something.
*I **never** drink alcohol.*
Adverbs of frequency usually go before the main verb but after the verb *be*.
*I like my teacher. She is **always** happy to help.*

I	am	always 100%	
You / We / They	are	usually often sometimes	late. watch TV.
He / She / It	is	never 0%	

Yes/No questions:
Do / Does + subject + adverb + verb.

Do Does	you she	usually sometimes	meet here? come here?

Wh- questions:
Wh- + *do / does* + subject + adverb + verb.

Where Why	do does	you he	usually always	meet? say yes?

1 Rearrange the words.

  a happy / am / always / I
  b TV / watches / never / she
  c usually / you / go out / do / at the weekend
  d he / does / work so hard / always / why
  e they / do / have problems with / what / usually

CAN / CAN'T FOR ABILITY

You use *can / cannot (can't)* to talk about what you are / aren't able to do.
*My brother **can** speak Arabic.*
*I **can't** play the violin.*

Subject + *can / cannot (can't)* + verb (without *to*)
There is no third person *-s* (He cans make decisions)

| I She | can | speak French |
| | cannot / can't | |

Questions and short answers
Can + subject + verb.

Can	you he	**lead** a team?

When a person asks a *can* question, you often answer with *Yes/No* + pronoun (he/she/it etc.) + *can / can't*.
Can you speak Russian? Yes, I can.
Can she play the guitar? No, she can't.

2 Write questions with *can*. Then use prompts to write short answers.

  a Can you / play the piano?   ✓
      Can you play the piano? Yes, I can.
  b you / work well under pressure ?   ✓
  c your mother / help you with your work ? ✗
  d your classmates / work well together ?   ✓
  e your father / speak French ?   ✗

UNIT 4 EDUCATION
PRESENT CONTINUOUS

You use the present continuous to talk about actions happening now.
*I'**m studying** design at the Edinburgh College of Art.*
You often use the present continuous with phrases and words like *at the moment* and *now*.
*I'**m (not) learning** a lot at the moment.*

Affirmative and negative

I	am ('m) / am not ('m not)	
You / We /They	are ('re) / are not (aren't)	working. studying.
He / She / It	is ('s) / is not (isn't)	

You often use contractions (*I'm, You're, She's* etc.) with the present continuous.
You don't usually use contractions in formal letters.

Questions and short answers

Am	I	
Are	you / we / they	**enjoying** life?
Is	he / she / it	

Yes/No + pronoun (she/we etc.) + *am / am not, are / aren't, is / isn't.*
Are you teaching English? No, I'm not.
Is your course interesting? Yes, it is.
You don't use contractions in affirmative short answers (Yes, I'm. / Yes, he's.)

Spelling

verbs ending with vowel + consonant + -e	verbs ending with vowel + consonant	verbs ending with vowel -y / -w
hope → hoping	win → winning	say → saying

1 Make sentences in the present continuous from the prompts. Use contractions where appropriate.

  a He / study / business
     He's studying business.
  b you / work / hard?
  c we / wait / for / his answer
  d they / plan / to stay / in Oman?
  e I / have / a good time / at the moment

PRESENT CONTINUOUS AND PRESENT SIMPLE

You use the present simple to talk about habits and things which are generally true.
It is important to have a good education.
You use the present continuous to talk about things which are happening now or changing.
The cost of education is going up.

2 Complete the sentences with the verb in brackets in the correct form.

  a Right now I *'m looking* (look) for a course in drama.
  b It _____ (cost) a lot of money to study in the US.
  c _____ you _____ (know) the answer?
  d Layla? She _____ (wash) her hair at the moment.
  e I _____ (be) at the station. I _____ (wait) for you!

Grammar reference

UNIT 5 BUILDINGS AND CITIES
PAST SIMPLE OF *BE*

The past of the verb be (*am / is / are*) is *was / were*.
He **was** an engineer. His parents **weren't** rich.

I He / She / It	**was / wasn't**	late for the
You / We / They	**were / weren't**	meeting.

Questions and short answers

Was	I / he / she / it	
Were	you / we / they	late again?

Yes/No + pronoun (*I/they* etc.) + *was / were*.
Yes, they were. / No, I wasn't.

Question words come before the verb.

What	was	it like?
How many rods	were	there?

1 Make sentences with *was, wasn't, were* and *weren't*.

   a there / (not) / many people / at the party
      There weren't many people at the party.
   b she / at school / today / ?
   c who / at the meeting / ?
   d how much / those shoes / ?
   e it / (not) / very warm / yesterday

PAST SIMPLE: REGULAR VERBS

You use the past simple to talk about actions and events that have finished. You form the regular past tense by adding *-d / -ed* to the verb.
*They **started** construction in 1853.*

| I / You / He / She / It / We / They | liked | the design. |
| | didn't like | |

Questions and short answers
Use the auxiliary verb *did* to form past simple questions and *didn't* for negatives.

Did	I / you / he / she / it / we / they	**like** it?

Yes/No + pronoun (*they/I* etc.) + *did / didn't*.
Yes, we did. / No, she didn't.

Question words come before the auxiliary.

When		they	build it?
Why	did	he	choose this design?

2 Complete the sentences with the past tense of the verb in brackets and the ✓ / ✗ prompt. Then write a question and short answer for each.

   a The baby _cried_ (cry). ✓
      Did the baby cry? Yes, it did.
   b They _didn't like_ (like) it. ✗
      Did they like it? No, they didn't.
   c We _____ (marry) in 2009. ✓
   d She _____ (want) a car. ✓
   e The police _____ (stop) him. ✓
   f You _____ (live) in Paris. ✗

UNIT 6 WORK
PAST SIMPLE QUESTIONS

Use the auxiliary verb *did* + subject + infinitive to form *Yes/No* past simple questions.
Did you **go** to university?

Did	I / you / he / she / it / we / they	**work** as a volunteer?

Short answers
Yes/No + I/You/(S)he/It/We/They + *did / didn't*
Yes, I did. / No, she didn't.

Question words come before the auxiliary.

What / When Where / Why What time How much	did	you she / it they	want to do? apply? study English? arrive? cost?

1 Make questions from the prompts.

   a you / meet / the volunteers?
   b when / they / arrive?
   c I / speak / to you / yesterday?
   d what / she / do / at the weekend?
   e how much / we / spend / on our last holiday?

PAST SIMPLE IRREGULAR VERBS

Irregular verbs do not have *-ed* endings. They all have different past tense forms.
Use *didn't* + infinitive to form the negative.
There is a full list of irregular verbs on page 144.

Infinitive	Past (+)	Past (-)
see	saw	didn't see
meet	met	didn't meet
get	got	didn't get
give	gave	didn't give
make	made	didn't make
leave	left	didn't leave
feel	felt	didn't feel
do	did	didn't do
find	found	didn't find
spend	spent	didn't spend
come	came	didn't come
stand	stood	didn't stand

Questions and short answers are formed in exactly the same way with regular verbs and irregular verbs (see top).

2 Complete the sentences with the irregular verbs in brackets in the correct form.

   a We _____ (have) a terrible holiday.
   b Sorry – I _____ (not see) you there.
   c It's okay, I _____ (find) my phone.
   d _____ (you meet) at university ?
   e He _____ (make) some mistakes, but he _____ (do) well.

UNIT 7 URBAN SPORTS
HAVE TO FOR OBLIGATION

You use *have to* to say you are obliged to do something.
*You **have to** solve all the clues.*

I / You / They / We	**have to**	work hard.
He / She / It	**has to**	

Questions and short answers

Do	I / you / we / they	**have to**	wear a uniform?
Does	he / she / it		be quick?

Yes/No + pronoun (I/he etc.) + do / does / don't / doesn't.
Do we have to go? Yes, you do. / No, you don't.

You use *don't have to* to say something is not necessary.
We don't have to go, but we can if we want.

I / You / They / We	**do not / don't**	**have to**	go.
He / She / It	**does not / doesn't**		

CAN / CAN'T FOR PERMISSION

You use *can / can't* to talk about what you are / aren't allowed to do.
***Can** I leave early today?*

I / You / He / She / It / We / They	**can** **can't (cannot)**	stay up late.

Questions and short answers

Can	you / she	leave early today?

Yes/No + pronoun (he/she/it etc.) + can / can't.
***Can** she take the afternoon off? No, she **can't**.*

1 Complete with the correct form of *can* or *have to*.

Zoe: [1] _____ I go out?
Dad: No, you [2] _____ . You [3] _____ do your homework.
Jack: Does she [4] _____ stay in all evening?
Dad: No, she [5] _____ stay in all evening. She [6] _____ go out when she finishes her homework. But you both [7] _____ be back here by eleven. OK?

NEED

You use *need* to say something is necessary.
*You **need** good walking shoes.*

Questions and short answers

Do	I / you / we / they	**need**		special clothes?
Does	he / she / it		to	be quick?

Yes/No + pronoun (she/it etc.) + do / does / don't / doesn't.

2 Complete the sentences with the correct form of *need*.

a <u>Do I need to</u> call you tomorrow?
b (she) _____ special equipment?
c (you) _____ come if you don't want to.
d I want to help but he says (he) _____ me.
e (they) _____ wake up very early on Saturday.

UNIT 8 THE NATURAL WORLD
PRESENT PERFECT SIMPLE + *EVER* & *NEVER*; PAST SIMPLE

You use the present perfect simple to talk about past experiences when you don't say exactly when they happened. You often use the present perfect with *ever* and *never*.
Have you ever seen a kangaroo?
No, I've never been to Australia.
Subject + auxiliary *have* + past participle

I / You / We / They	**have ('ve) (never)** **haven't**	**been to** **visited**	Fiji.
He / She / It	**has ('s) (never)** **hasn't**		

Question and short answers

Have **Has**	you she	**(ever) been** **(ever) tried**	to India? Japanese food?

Yes/No + pronoun (I/he etc.) + have / has / haven't / hasn't.
Yes, I have. / No, she hasn't.

You use the past simple to talk about the past when you want to give specific details, such as when, where, who with, etc. We often use the past simple with a time expression.

I / You / We / They	**went to / didn't go to**	Fiji	last year two years ago in June.
He / She / It	**visited / didn't visit**		with Ruby.

Question and short answers

Did	you she we they	**go to** **visit**	Fiji	last year? two years ago? in June?
				with Ruby?

Yes/No + pronoun (I/he etc.) + did / didn't
Yes, I did. / No, she didn't.

1 Make three-line dialogues from the prompts.

a **A** you / go to / Egypt? **B** Yes **A** When?
   A <u>Have you been to Egypt?</u> **B** <u>Yes, I have.</u>
   A <u>When did you go?</u>
b **A** he / try / Korean food? **B** Yes **A** When?
c **A** she / meet / popstar? **B** Yes – Jay-Z **A** When?
d **A** you / (ever) do / dangerous sport? **B** No, never.

PRESENT PERFECT WITH *FOR* AND *SINCE*

You use the present perfect to talk about something which began in the past and continues up to now, with a present result. *Eighteen species of mammal have become extinct.*

You use *for* when you give the period of time. You use *since* when you give the beginning of the time.
*I've known him **for** ten years. We've been friends **since** 2005.*

2 Choose the correct answers.

a We've lived here *for / since* a year.
b We haven't heard from them *for / since* Monday.
c They've been in Cyprus *for / since* 2010.
d He's been my friend *for / since* we were children.
e You haven't seen them *for / since* a long time.

Grammar reference **141**

Grammar reference

Unit 9 Family
Present simple passive

You form the present simple passive with the present of the verb *be* + the past participle.
*The babies **are given** presents.*
You can use *by* to say who or what does something.
*Each egg **is painted** red **by** the parents.*

I You / We / They He / She / It	am / am not are / aren't is / isn't	invited. given presents.

Questions and short answers

Am Are Is	I you / we / they he / she / it	invited given a gift	(by the parents?)

Yes/No + pronoun (I/he etc.) + *am / am not, are / aren't, is / isn't*
Yes, I am. / No, she isn't.

1   Complete the sentences with the verbs in brackets in the present simple passive.
   a   The party _____ (hold) on the baby's first birthday.
   b   A present _____ (give) to each guest.
   c   Special cakes _____ (eat) by the guests.
   d   The colour red _____ (consider) lucky in China.
   e   A girl's fifteenth birthday _____ (celebrate) in Chile.

Passive and active

In an active sentence, the performer of the action is usually the subject (*They* in the example).
***They grow** fruit in the valley.*
When the performer of the action is not considered important, you can make the object of the sentence (*fruit*) into the subject and change the verb form. This is called a passive sentence.
*Fruit **is grown** in the valley.*

Active

Subject	Verb	Object
They They	spend eat	their lives on the move. each plant raw.

Passive

Subject	*be*	Past participle
Their lives Each plant	are is	spent on the move. eaten raw.

2   Order the words to make sentences. Then tick (✓) the passive sentences.
   a   worn / by / kimonos / usually / women / are / young
   b   their / moving / spend / they / lives / around
   c   given / people / get older / are / as they / more respect
   d   a lot of / they / and vegetables / eat / fruit
   e   are / healthy / they / lifestyle / known / their / for

Unit 10 Conservation
Countable and uncountable nouns / *some* and *any*

Countable nouns have a plural and a singular form.
(There is a) tree / (There are two) trees
Uncountable nouns only have a singular form.
(There is some) litter.

1   Write the nouns below under the correct heading.

water   people   river   problem   rain   year   time
music   food   poster   money   tree   coffee   idea

Countable	Uncountable

You use *some* and *any* with countable and uncountable nouns. You use *some* with statements.
*We saw **some** people we know.*
You use *any* with questions and negatives.
*Are there **any** students here?*
*There isn't **any** milk left.*

+	There	is	a **some**	tree. (countable singular) money. (uncountable)
		are	**some**	trees. (countable plural)
–		isn't	a **any**	tree. (countable singular) money. (uncountable)
		aren't	**any**	trees. (countable plural)

Question and short answers

Are Is	there	any	people? / posters? food? / music?

Yes/No + there + *is / isn't, are / aren't.*
Yes, there are. / No, there isn't.

2   Complete the sentences with *some* or *any*.
   a   Is everything okay – are there _____ problems?
   b   There is _____ coffee but no tea, I'm afraid.
   c   There aren't _____ trees in our garden.
   d   There are _____ people at the door.
   e   Is there _____ rain at this time of year?

HOW MUCH / HOW MANY

You use *how many* with countable nouns and *how much* with uncountable nouns when you want to ask questions about quantity.
***How many** rivers are polluted?*
***How much** rain do you have in a year?*

3   Choose the correct answers.
   a   How *much / many* money do you have?
   b   Do you know how *much / many* time we have left?
   c   How *much / many* people were at the party?
   d   How *much / many* years have you lived here?
   e   We need to know how *much / many* food there is.

UNIT 11 DESIGN
COMPARATIVES

To compare two things you use a comparative adjective + *than*.
*His car is **faster than** the others.*
*He is a **more dangerous** driver **than** his teammate.*

1	Add *-r* or *-er* to one-syllable adjectives.	**safer** **faster**
2	Double the consonant and add *-er* to adjectives ending in consonant – vowel – consonant.	**bigger** **thinner**
3	Add *-ier* to adjectives ending in *-y*.	**easier** **busier**
4	Use *more* + adjective for longer adjectives.	**more dangerous**
5	Irregular adjectives (good, bad, far)	**better, worse, further**

1 **Complete the sentences with the adjectives in brackets in the comparative form.**

  a Molly is _____ (good) at maths _____ Jack.
  b Our new house is a lot _____ (big) our old house.
  c Driving to Italy is _____ (expensive) flying.
  d Raw vegetables are _____ (healthy) cooked ones.
  e I am _____ (tall) my brother.

SUPERLATIVES

To compare more than two things you use *the* + a superlative adjective. Superlative adjectives show the greatest quality.
*His car is **the fastest** in the competition.*
*He was **the most dangerous** driver in the race.*

1	Add *-st* or *-est* to one-syllable adjectives.	**the safest** **the fastest**
2	Double the consonant and add *-est* to adjectives ending in consonant – vowel – consonant.	**the biggest** **the thinnest**
3	Add *-iest* to adjectives ending in *-y*.	**the easiest** **the busiest**
4	Use the *most* + adjective for longer adjectives.	**the most experienced**
5	Irregular adjectives (good, bad, far)	**the best, the worst, the furthest**

2 **Make sentences from the prompts. Change the adjective to the superlative form.**

  a It / is / safe / sport / I've ever tried
  b She / is / beautiful / woman / in the world
  c Who / is / good / football team / in your country?
  d I'm / fat / person / at our gym
  e They / are / friendly / people / I've ever met

Now rewrite each sentence, changing the adjective to its opposite.

UNIT 12 PLANS AND PREDICTIONS
GOING TO

You use (*be*) *going to* + verb (infinitive) to talk about your future hopes, wishes and plans.
I'm going to work in South Africa.

Affirmative and negative

I	**am ('m)** **am not ('m not)**		go.
You /We They	**are ('re)** **are not (aren't)**	**going to**	work. do it.
He / She / It	**is ('s)** **is not (isn't)**		

You often use contractions (I'm, You're, She's etc.) when making sentences using *going to*.

Questions and short answers

Am	I		
Are	you / we / they	**going to**	see Sue today?
Is	he / she / it		

Yes/No + pronoun + am / am not, are / aren't, is / isn't.
Are you going to join us? No, I'm not. / Yes, we are.

Wh- questions
Question words come before the auxiliary (*am, is, are*).
What are we going to do?

1 **Make statements and questions with *going to*.**

  a you / stay at home / this weekend?
  b she / (not) finish / her course
  c when / they / go / to Japan?
  d I / travel round Europe / for three months

WILL / WON'T

When you want to make predictions about the future, use *will, will not* or *won't*.
*Students **will** do their classes online.*
*We **won't** spend much time at school.*

I, You, He, She, It, We, They	**will ('ll)**	pay more for education
	will not / won't	

Questions and short answers
Will + subject + verb.

Will	I, you, he, she, it, we, they	go to libraries?

Yes/No + pronoun (he/she/it etc.) + will / will not (won't)
Question words come before *will*. *Where will we work?*

2 **Write sentences using *will* or *won't*.**

  a Students / go to school ✗
     Students won't go to school.
  b Education / be like a business ✓
  c Private companies / own schools ✓
  d Governments / control schools ✗
  e Students / have to take exams ✗

3 **Now write a question and short answer for each statement.**

  a *Will students go to school? No, they won't.*

Grammar reference **143**

Irregular verbs

Infinitive	Past simple	Past participle
be	was/were	been
become	became	become
begin	began /bɪgæn/	begun /bɪgʌn/
bet	bet	bet
bite /baɪt/	bit	bitten /bɪtən/
blow /bləʊ/	blew /bluː/	blown /bləʊn/
break	broke	broken
bring	brought /brɔːt/	brought
build /bɪld/	built /bɪlt/	built
burn	burnt	burnt
buy	bought /bɔːt/	bought
catch	caught /kɔːt/	caught
choose	chose /tʃəʊz/	chosen
come	came	come
cost	cost	cost
cut	cut	cut
do	did	done
draw /drɔː/	drew /druː/	drawn /drɔːn/
dream	dreamt	dreamt
drink	drank/dræŋk/	drunk /drʌŋk/
drive	drove	driven
eat	ate /eɪt/	eaten /iːtən/
fall /fɔːl/	fell /fel/	fallen /fɔːlən/
feel /fiːl/	felt /felt/	felt
fight /faɪt/	fought /fɔːt/	fought
find	found /faʊnd/	found
flee	flew	flown
fly /flaɪ/	flew /fluː/	flown /fləʊn/
forget	forgot	forgotten
forgive	forgave	forgiven
freeze	froze	frozen
get	got	got
give	gave	given
go	went	been/gone
grow /grəʊ/	grew /gruː/	grown /grəʊn/
hang /hæŋ/	hung /hʌŋ/	hung
have	had	had
hear /hɪə/	heard /hɜːd/	heard /hɜːd/
hide	hid	hidden /hɪdən/
hit	hit	hit
hold	held	held
hurt /hɜːt/	hurt	hurt
keep	kept	kept
know /nəʊ/	knew /njuː/	known /nəʊn/
lay /leɪ/	laid	laid
lead /liːd/	led /led/	led
learn /lɜːn/	learnt	learnt
leave	left	left
lend	lent	lent

Infinitive	Past simple	Past participle
let	let	let
lie	lay	lain
lie (not tell the truth)	lied	lied
lose /luːz/	lost	lost
make	made	made
mean	meant	meant
meet	met	met
pay /peɪ/	paid /peɪd/	paid
prove	proved	proven/proved
put	put	put
read /riːd/	read /red/	read /red/
ride	rode	ridden
ring	rang /ræŋ/	rung /rʌŋ/
run /rʌn/	ran /ræn/	run
say /seɪ/	said /sed/	said
see	saw /sɔː/	seen
sell	sold	sold
send	sent	sent
set	set	set
shoot	shot	shot
show	showed	shown
shut	shut	shut
sing	sang /sæŋ/	sung /sʌŋ/
sink	sank /sæŋk/	sunk /sʌŋk/
sit	sat	sat
sleep	slept	slept
slide	slid	slid
speak	spoke	spoken
spell	spelt	spelt
spend	spent	spent
spoil	spoilt	spoilt
spread /spred/	spread	spread
stand	stood	stood
steal	stole	stolen
stick	stuck /stʌk/	stuck
strike /straɪk/	struck /strʌk/	struck
swear	swore	sworn
swim	swam /swæm/	swum /swʌm/
take /teɪk/	took /tʊk/	taken /teɪkən/
teach	taught /tɔːt/	taught
tell	told	told
think	thought /θɔːt/	thought
throw /θrəʊ/	threw /θruː/	thrown /θrəʊn/
understand	understood	understood
wake	woke /wəʊk/	woken /wəʊkən/
wear /weə/	wore /wɔː/	worn /wɔːn/
win	won /wʌn/	won
write	wrote	written /rɪtən/